French Grammar

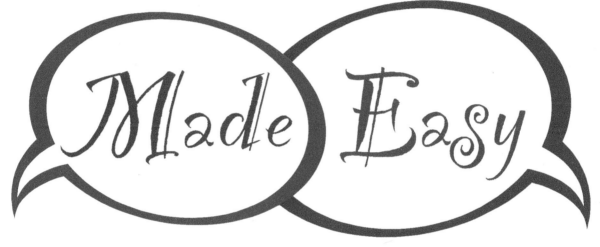

Made Easy

C'est facile !

Claire Redmond

First published 2009
The Educational Company of Ireland
Ballymount Road
Walkinstown
Dublin 12

A member of the Smurfit Kappa Group PLC

Design and layout: Identikit Design Consultants
Cover design: Identikit Design Consultants
Editor: Linda Longmore
Language coordinator: Diane Kennedy
Artist: Kim Shaw

Photograph credits
Shutterstock

08A15

Contents

Preface

A new book designed to make grammar easy and build students confidence in the area. The vibrant, colourful design is complemented by easy to understand explanations and a user-friendly format.

- French grammar presented in a clear, fun and fresh format

- Simple explanations look at grammar from a student's point of view using relevant, interesting examples throughout

- Tips and advice provided for completing exercises

- Key grammatical points that students find difficult and puzzling are explained in fun and novel ways

- Simplifies some of the more difficult grammar issues

- Confidence building – engages with the students on their level

- Free teacher's CD which contains supplementary work and answers

Acknowledgements

This book is dedicated to my parents.
Mam and Dad, **impossible n'est pas français**, there is no such word as can't.

I would like to thank all those who have helped me so much, in so many ways:

- To Barry and John for the support and good humour.

- To Biddy for the prayers and **café au lait**.

- To my fantastic friends and cousins, for their endless supply of time.

- To my great students and colleagues, past and present in Maryfield College, Drumcondra.

- To all at Edco for their advice and enthusiasm.

The Story of French

French, like Italian and Spanish, is known as one of the Romance languages. 'Romance' in this sense has a different meaning than what we are used to! French is a descendant of the Latin language of the Roman Empire, which is the *roman* in *romance*.

So, what do you need to know about French? Students often ask, *but why?* in response to some of the rules in French. Like any language, French has its rules and regulations. English, which most of you speak on a daily basis, is actually very difficult to learn. For example, in French you only have to learn one present tense, whereas in English you must learn two! Let's take the verb **donner** *to give*. **Je donne** means *I give, I do give* and *I am giving*.

French is spoken by around 200 million francophones (French-speaking people) in countries spread across five continents of the world. You might wonder why French is spoken in so many far away places. There was always huge rivalry between European nations to gain more territory and France was a very powerful nation, gaining land through war, peace agreements and by colonisation, where French settlers were placed in the country France had taken over.

This is why if you go to Canada, for example, you will hear French, but it sounds very different from the French you hear in Paris.

Although the French use the same alphabet as us, you will notice accents on some of the letters. Let's take a look them.

- The accent **aigu** (é) is used in French.

- The accent **grave** (à, è, ù) is also used.

- The **circonflexe** (â, ê, î, ô, û) can be used on any of the five vowels.

- The **tréma** accent occurs in very few words. It shows that two vowels beside each other must be pronounced. Two examples of its use are in the words naïve, which we have taken as our own word in English, *naïve*, and the French-made car **Citroën**.

- The final accent is called **cedille** and is only found on the letter *c*, like this, **ç**. It indicates that it should be pronounced softly, like *s*, rather than *k*. Probably one of the first things you learned in French was the expression **Ça va ?** *How are you*? Remember how it's pronounced?

Now let's also have a look at some of the people, things and symbols you will be meeting as you work through this book.

Consider Pépé to be your best friend in this book as he encourages and helps you along the way.

Alan and Amy feature throughout the book. Amy likes Alan. Alan, while liking Amy, likes football and chatting with his friends more! Follow their story throughout the book.

This sign means you have learned this particular point and you will now need to use it again.

This sign means you may need to stop, think this point out and read it again, as understanding it will really help you.

This sign means you need to learn the topic by heart.

Chapter 1
Les Articles et les Noms
Articles and Nouns

Key words

- ···⟫ Nouns
- ···⟫ Articles
- ···⟫ Gender

- ···⟫ The definite article
- ···⟫ The indefinite article
- ···⟫ The partitive article
- ···⟫ Negative

1.1 Nouns

Sometimes students of French become confused about articles because these have to agree with the noun they are 'attached' to.

It might be a good idea to clarify what a noun is before we proceed:

Nouns are words that name people, animals or things.

In French, all nouns are divided into two groups: masculine nouns and feminine nouns. When you look up a word in the dictionary, you will be given an indication as to whether it is masculine or feminine.

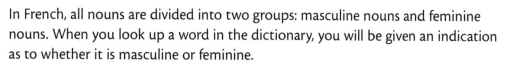

nf = noun feminine, **nm** = noun masculine

You also need to check/learn/revise/relearn those vocabulary lists that your teacher made you painstakingly note down!

The general rule in French is that if you have a noun, there is an article before it. This little word indicates whether a noun is feminine, masculine or plural.

There is no definite way to know whether a noun is masculine or feminine, but some tips will be included to help you work it out!

1.2 So, what is an article?

There are *three* kinds of articles in French:

1 Definite
2 Indefinite
3 Partitive

1.3 Definite articles

The definite article in French corresponds to *the* in English. There are four forms of it:

Masculine	Feminine	Before a vowel or silent 'h'	All Plurals	
Le garçon	**La** fille	**L'**oncle	**Les** chats	**Les** garçons
Le père	**La** mère	**L'**animal	**Les** crayons	**Les** filles

Exercise 1

Choose the correct form of the definite article **le**, **la**, **l'** or **les** in these sentences. Remember to use your dictionary or your vocabulary lists if you are not sure!

1 J'aime lire dans _____ train.

2 _____ école s'appelle St Aidan's.

3 _____ magasins sont près de chez moi.

4 _____ porte est ouverte.

5 _____ femmes sont belles.

6 Nous allons à _____ plage.

7 J'habite à _____ campagne.

8 _____ chien est mignon !

9 Nous restons dans _____hôtel.

10 Je nage dans _____ mer.

1.4 Indefinite articles

Now that you know what the **definite** article is, what do you think its opposite form is?

Of course, it is **a**! This is **indefinite**, so instead of saying *the* girl, if we are not sure which girl it is exactly, we say *a* girl.

Instead of the plural **les**, meaning *the* for plural nouns, we have **des** which means *some*.

Table of indefinite articles:

Masculine	Feminine	All Plurals	
Un garçon	**Une** fille	**Des** chats	**Des** garçons
Un père	**Une** mère	**Des** crayons	**Des** filles

There is no shortened form of the indefinite article in front of a vowel or silent h.

e.g. L'école   *the school*
      une école   *a school*

Exercise 2

Choose the correct form of the indefinite article **un**, **une** or **des** in the following sentences:

1 J'habite dans _____ grande ville.

2 Mon ami Derek habite dans _____ petit village.

3 Est-ce qu'il y a _____ supermarché près d'ici ?

4 Puis-je prendre _____ douche, s'il vous plaît ?

5 Je voudrais _____ sandwich.

6 Nous devons porter _____ chemises blanches.

7 Ma mère travaille dans _____ bureau.

8 J'ai _____ chien qui s'appelle Benny.

9 Il y a _____ vélos à louer.

10 Mes amis ont _____ ordinateurs portables.

1.5 The partitive article

The partitive article corresponds to the idea of *some* or *any* in English. There are four forms of the French partitive article:

Masculine	Feminine	Before a vowel or silent 'h'	All Plurals
Du pain	**De la** glace	**De l'**eau	**Des** bananes
Du café	**De la** viande	**De l'**huile	**Des** champignons

Note:
The indefinite article and the partitive article both have the same word, **des**, in the plural.

Pronunciation
les and **des** are pronounced *lay* and *day*.

When you want to say *some* or *any*, you use the partitive article:

Example:	Je voudrais des oranges.	*I'd like some oranges.*
or	Je voudrais du pain.	*I'd like some bread.*

In English we often leave this out. However, in French we must always include it.

Est-ce que tu as **des** projets pour les vacances ?	*Have you plans for the holidays?*
Je mange de la glace.	*I am eating some ice cream.*

Let's face it, much as you might like to, you can't eat all the ice cream in the world so you just have *some!*

Let's illustrate the difference. You can eat a slice of chocolate cake, some chocolate cake, or the whole thing.

Je bois du café.	*I drink/am drinking some coffee.*
J'ai de l'argent.	*I have some money.*

(Not all the money in the world, but *some* of the money, even if is just €5!)

Have you noticed that the *some* idea is really important when talking about food, drink, or money?

If, however, you want to make a general statement about chocolate and say that you quite simply love it (whatever brand, milky or dark!), you then go back to the definite article and say:

J'adore le chocolat.	*I love chocolate.*

1.6 De and the negative

After a negative, a simpler form of **du/de la/de l'/des** is used. It is one simple word, **de**.

Example:

Je bois du café/Je ne bois pas **de** café.
I drink/I don't drink coffee.

Tu manges du pain ?/Je ne mange pas **de** pain.
Do you eat bread?/I do not eat bread.

Tu bois du thé ?/Je ne bois pas **de** thé.
Do you drink tea?/I do not drink tea.

Tu manges des croissants ?/Je ne mange pas **de** croissants.
Do you eat croissants?/I do not eat croissants.

Tu veux de l'eau ?/Non, je ne veux pas **d'**eau.
Do you want water?/No, I do not want water.

Tu achètes des oranges?/Non, je n'achète pas **d'**oranges.
Are you buying oranges?/No, I am not buying oranges.

Rappel !

Remember **de** becomes **d'** before a vowel!

Exercise 3

Write the correct form of the partitive article **du**, **de la**, **de l'**, **des**, or **de** in the following sentences:

1 Je ne prends pas _____ sucre dans mon thé.

2 Je ne bois pas _____ eau.

3 Ils boivent _____ thé au restaurant.

4 Je prends _____ viande.

5 Je ne veux pas _____ légumes.

6 Elle mange _____ chocolat tout le temps.

7 Je voudrais _____ renseignements sur Paris.

8 J'ai un petit boulot pour gagner _____ argent.

9 Chez moi, nous ne mangeons pas _____ frites.

10 Est-ce que tu as _____ projets pour l'été ?

Exercise 4

Now let's put them all together! Decide which article is most appropriate in the following sentences and then circle it. Test yourself. Do a quick revision of your vocabulary, particularly on food and classroom items.

1 J'adore *la/une/de la* mousse au chocolat.

2 Je voudrais *la/de la/une* banane.

3 Sarah mange *les/des* fraises.

4 Où est *la/une/du* télécommande ?

5 Je prends *du/le/un* lait avec les céréales.

6 Tous *les/des* étudiants passent leurs examens.

7 Il y a *un/le/du* homme à la porte.

8 Mangez-vous *les/des* légumes ?

9 Je n'ai pas *un/d'/du* ordinateur.

10 Mon père va acheter *une/la/de la* nouvelle voiture.

11 Mes parents n'achètent pas *de/des/les* frites.

12 Mon voisin a *un/le/du* chat.

13 Est-ce que vous mangez *du/le/un* pain au petit déjeuner ?

14 Est-ce que tu veux *de l'/ l'/une* eau.

15 Donnez-moi *le/du/un* beurre, s'il vous plaît.

16 J'ai *des/d'/ les* amis qui habitent en France.

17 Est-ce que vous avez *du/de/un* temps pour m'aider ?

18 Le samedi matin nous prenons *le/de/du* petit déjeuner au café.

19 Mon frère ne boit pas *du/un/de* lait.

20 Les étudiants travaillent pour gagner *de/de l'/du* argent.

1.7 Gender of nouns – how do we know?

What is so masculine or feminine about nouns?

It is easy to understand why the word for man, a boy, a father or an uncle should be masculine or why the word for woman, a daughter, a grandmother or a mother should be feminine.

On the other hand, why should a book be masculine? Why should a door be feminine?

What are the reasons behind gender in French? There is no definite answer. You must learn to *associate and visualise* the proper article with the noun you are learning.

There are, however, some patterns in word endings – certain endings tend to indicate masculine nouns, while other endings tend to be for feminine nouns. This is not fool proof, but they can help you to figure out the gender of many French nouns.

The following endings usually indicate that the noun is **feminine**:

-elle	-ienne	-ière
-ette	-euse	-onne

1.8 Feminine nouns

In French, as in English, we have feminine forms of the noun.

To make a noun feminine, the general rule is you add **-e** to the masculine singular form.

Example: un voisin   **une** voisine

Some nouns are a little peculiar.

-eur	⋯▶	-euse	Le chanteur	La chanteuse	*the singer*
-er	⋯▶	-ère	Le fermier	La fermière	*the farmer*
-ien	⋯▶	-ienne	L'italien	L'italienne	*the Italian*
-teur	⋯▶	-trice	l'acteur	l'actrice	*the actor/actress*

And yes, some are just downright odd! Remember, though, we can have a completely different word in English too. Take a look at the third column below:

Masculine word	Feminine word	English words
Un garçon	Une fille	*Boy/girl*
Un héros	Une héroïne	*Hero/heroine*
Un homme	Une femme	*Man/woman*
Un mari	Une femme	*Husband/wife*
Un monsieur	Une dame	*Gentleman/lady*
Un neveu	Une nièce	*Nephew/niece*
Un oncle	Une tante	*Uncle/aunt*
Un parrain	Une marraine	*Godfather/godmother*
Un roi	Une reine	*King/queen*
Un vieillard	Une vieille	*Old man/woman*

Test yourself on this one! Study the table on page 12 for five minutes. Write down what you are probably muttering in your head. It tends to 'stick' easier this way!

Now, cover the second and third columns and see if you can remember the feminine word and what it means in English.

1.9 Plural nouns

1 Normally, nouns are made plural by adding **s**.

Le café	⋯⋮	Les café**s**	⋯⋮	*the café/cafés* **or** *the coffee/coffees*
L'école	⋯⋮	Les école**s**	⋯⋮	*the school/schools*

2 Nouns which end in **s**, **x** or **z** in the singular, do not change.

Le fils	⋯⋮	Les fils	⋯⋮	*the son/sons*
La voix	⋯⋮	Les voix	⋯⋮	*the voice/voices*
Le nez	⋯⋮	Les nez	⋯⋮	*the nose/noses*

3 Nouns which end in **-au** and **-eu** in the singular, add an **x** in the plural.

Le jeu	⋯⋮	Les jeu**x**	⋯⋮	*the game/games*
Le cadeau	⋯⋮	Les cadeau**x**	⋯⋮	*the present/presents*

Exception:

le pneu	⋯⋮	les pneu**s**	⋯⋮	*the tyre/tyres*

4 Nouns which end in **-al** in the singular, change the **-al** to **-aux**.

Le journal	⋯⋮	Les journ**aux**	⋯⋮	*the newspaper/newspapers*
Le cheval	⋯⋮	Les chev**aux**	⋯⋮	*the horse/horses*

Exceptions:

Le bal	⋯⋮	Les bal**s**	⋯⋮	*the ball/balls*
Le carnaval	⋯⋮	Les carnaval**s**	⋯⋮	*the carnival/carnivals*

5 Nouns ending in **-ou** in the singular, take **-s** in the plural:

Le cou	⋯⟩	les cous	⋯⟩	*the neck/necks*
Le trou	⋯⟩	les trous	⋯⟩	*the hole/holes*

Exceptions:

Le bijou	⋯⟩	Les bijoux	⋯⟩	*the jewel/jewels*
Le genou	⋯⟩	Les genoux	⋯⟩	*the knee/knees*

6 There are a few nouns which have irregular plurals.

Un œil	⋯⟩	Des yeux	⋯⟩	*the eye/eyes*
Monsieur	⋯⟩	Messieurs	⋯⟩	*sir/sirs, gentleman/gentlemen*
Madame	⋯⟩	Mesdames	⋯⟩	*lady/ladies*
Le ciel	⋯⟩	Les cieux	⋯⟩	*the sky/skies*

7 Family names do not change in the plural:

Les Dubois

Les Guillaume

8 There are some nouns which are often used *only in the plural*:

Les cheveux (*hair*), les vacances (*holidays*), les devoirs (*homework*).

Exercise 5

Write the nouns in brackets in the plural.

1 J'ai trois (frère) _____ et deux (sœur) _____.

2 Mes tantes aiment faire les (magasin) _____.

3 Mes amis me donnent beaucoup de (cadeau) _____ pour
mon anniversaire.

4 Ma sœur Jodie a les (œil) _____ bleus.

5 J'aime les (bijou) _____.

6 Nous avons trois (animal) _____ chez nous.

7 Andy s'est blessé aux deux (genou) _____ en jouant au basket.

8 Les (rideau) _____ sont rouges dans ma chambre.

9 En vacances en Italie, nous avons visité plusieurs (château) _____.

10 Mon oncle lit beaucoup de (journal) _____ le dimanche.

1.10 Some things you should note

Sometimes in French articles are used when in English they are not.

With parts of the body:	Je me brosse **les** cheveux.	⋯▷	*I brush my hair.*

*In English we use a possessive adjective – more about those later! See page 39.

Names of countries:	**L'**Irlande	⋯▷	*Ireland*
	La France	⋯▷	*France*
	L'Italie	⋯▷	*Italy*

Names of languages:	**L'**irlandais	⋯▷	*Irish*
	L'anglais	⋯▷	*English*
	Le français	⋯▷	*French*

Names of games:	**Le** basket	⋯▷	*basketball*
	Le tennis	⋯▷	*tennis*
	Le foot	⋯▷	*football*

Names of school subjects:	**Le** dessin	⋯▷	*art*
	La biologie	⋯▷	*biology*
	Les maths	⋯▷	*maths*

Rappel !

One other thing to note. The article is not used in French with a person's profession.

Je suis professeur.	*I am a teacher.*
Simon est comptable.	*Simon is an accountant.*

So there we go! Now you need to think back on this chapter and make sure you can truthfully put a tick beside each item on this checklist:

Récapitulez

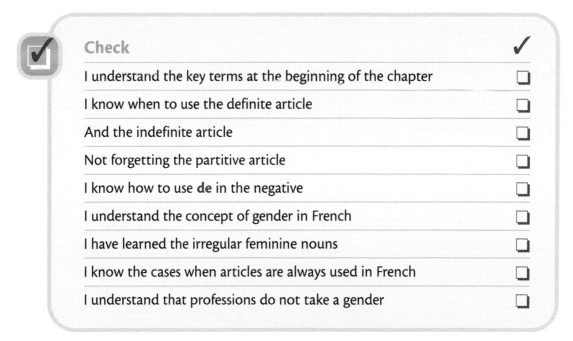

Check	✔
I understand the key terms at the beginning of the chapter	☐
I know when to use the definite article	☐
And the indefinite article	☐
Not forgetting the partitive article	☐
I know how to use **de** in the negative	☐
I understand the concept of gender in French	☐
I have learned the irregular feminine nouns	☐
I know the cases when articles are always used in French	☐
I understand that professions do not take a gender	☐

Chapter 2
Les Adjectifs
Adjectives

Key words

- Modify
- Gender
- Agreement
- Invariable
- Comparative
- Superlative

- Demonstrative
- Suffix
- Interrogative
- Possessive
- Context

2.1 A quick word before we begin

French adjectives are fascinating little things really.

Did you know about adjectives?

Fact One
In English, adjectives are usually found in front of the noun, but most French adjectives follow the noun they modify (or tell you more about),
e.g. Le livre bleu

Fact Two
In French, adjectives change in gender and number with the nouns that they modify, e.g. Le chien noir, les portes noir**es**.

Fact Three
If the feminine singular adjective ends in **-e**, no change occurs,
e.g. **facile** (*easy*) is the same in the masculine and feminine forms.

Fact Four

Yes, there are irregular ones. Yes, some do come after the noun. Yes, some are very strange and have special forms. These peculiar creatures have a special singular form before a noun beginning with a vowel or a silent *h*.

These are the four key facts you need to keep in mind as we progress. One other tip: Learn the various sections, **par cœur**, little by little. Everything will *stick* in your mind a lot easier this way.

As adjectives go hand-in-hand with the nouns they describe, you may already know the vocabulary in this chapter. If not, make sure to check your dictionary for new words. Just to be fully prepared for this chapter, you should revise your vocabulary for:

- school
- the classroom and subjects
- family
- morning, afternoon, evening, week, year
- pets
- times
- house

2.2 Introducing/defining adjectives

An adjective is a word that describes a noun.

Sometimes you hear this explanation slightly differently. You might hear that an adjective *modifies* a noun, or an adjective tells us more about a noun,

e.g. a *green* gate, a *happy* student, *my* dog.

Essentially, however, it is the same thing. Adjectives simply give us more information about a noun.

Let's take a look at a break down of a sentence.

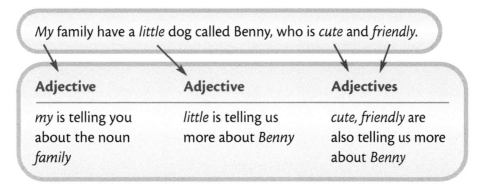

My family have a *little* dog called Benny, who is *cute* and *friendly*.

Adjective	Adjective	Adjectives
my is telling you about the noun *family*	*little* is telling us more about *Benny*	*cute, friendly* are also telling us more about *Benny*

So in English, remember that the most obvious adjectives tend to be before the noun, but they can come after it too. Words like *my* and *your* are also adjectives, known as **possessive adjectives**, but more about those later.

2.3 Adjectives already ending in *-e*

If the adjective already ends in **-e**, no changes are necessary for the feminine form.

Example: jaune *(yellow)*   rouge *(red)*   jeune *(young)*

Example:
Le rideau jaune	*the yellow curtain*
La lampe jaune	*the yellow lamp*
Le jeune garçon	*the young boy*
La jeune fille	*the young girl*

2.4 Agreement of adjectives

In French, an adjective that goes with a noun must agree with that noun in gender and number. Put simply, we need to consider whether the noun is masculine or feminine and whether we are talking about one or more than one. As we mentioned, the general rules are:

- Add **e** to form the feminine singular.
- To make an adjective masculine plural, add **s** to the masculine singular form.
- To make it feminine plural, add **es** to the masculine singular form.

Remember, before you can use **un adjectif**, you must check the gender and number. Let's take the example of the colour green, **vert**.

The pronunciation changes here when you add the **e** to make the feminine form. We pronounce the **te** in **verte**, whereas in the masculine **vert** we don't pronounce the **t**.

	Singular	Plural
Masc	vert	verts
Fem	verte	vertes

Tip:
This rule applies to adjectives that end in most consonants (the letters that aren't vowels!) as well as those that end with **é**.

Now look at it with some nouns.
We'll take the example of **le livre** (*the book*) and **la porte** (*the door*).

Masculine singular	Masculine plural	Feminine singular	Feminine plural
le livre vert	les livres verts	la porte verte	les portes vertes
the green book	*the green books*	*the green door*	*the green doors*

Points to note

1 Colours and nationalities will always come after the noun.

Example:

La chaise noire	the black chair
Les rideaux bleus	the blue curtains
Une fille française	a French girl
Un homme irlandais	an Irish man

Non !

2 Invariable adjectives (or adjectives that simply refuse to change!)

Remember when you are describing what people look like that neither **marron** *(brown)*, nor **noisette** *(hazel coloured)*, take an **s** in the plural.

> **Adjectives like this are said to be invariable; they don't agree in gender or number.**

Note:
Cheveux is plural because remember you have more than one hair on your head!

Example:

	les yeux bleus	blue eyes
but	les yeux marron	brown eyes or
	les yeux noisette	hazel-coloured eyes

les cheveux bruns is used for *brown hair.*

And while we're on the subject, let's add a little more to this point:

When adjectives are actually the names of flowers, fruits and jewels (e.g. hazel, chestnut, orange, emerald), they work like the examples above and there is no agreement in gender or number.

> Example: Les filles portent des robes orange.

Des robes, (*dresses*), is feminine plural; **orange** does not agree, however, because it is the name of a fruit.

> Example: Les boucles d'oreilles **émeraude** sont belles.

Des boucles d'oreilles (*earrings*) are feminine plural. An emerald is a jewel or precious stone, so **émeraude** does not agree.

> Example: Ma grand-mère tricote des pulls lavande.

Des pulls, (*jumpers*) are masculine plural; **lavande** as it comes originally from the name of a plant does not change.

The exception to this is **rose** (*pink*), which we make plural by adding an **s** as is usual with adjectives, even though the word obviously comes from the flower.

> Example: Elle porte toujours des vêtements **roses**.
> *She always wears pink clothes.*

3 **Compound adjectives (where you have two adjectives together)**

   a) If the two adjectives are two colours, neither agrees in gender or number with the noun:

> Example: Les chemises **rose pale**   *pale pink shirts*

Rose pale, (*pale pink*) does not change to agree with the plural, **chemises** (*shirts*).

Example: Les chemises vert pomme *apple green shirts*

vert pomme, *(apple green)* does not change to agree with the plural **chemises** *(shirts)*.

b) If the compound adjective is made up of a word that doesn't change (remember, we say it is *invariable*) and an adjective, only the adjective agrees. Let's take the example of **avant-dernier**, *(second last)*. The word **avant** does not change. If you look it up in your dictionary you will see it has the word **prép** beside it, meaning it is a preposition, so it has no business at all changing! The word **dernier**, which is an adjective, will agree with the noun though.

Example: Elle est arrivée l'avant-dernière à la course.
She finished second last in the race.

c) If the compound adjective is made up of two adjectives that are not colours, they agree in gender and in number with the noun. Take for example *sweet and sour* or **aigre-doux**. You might use this sauce on potatoes to make them tastier, giving you:

Example: Des pommes de terre aigres-douces *sweet and sour potatoes*

See how **aigre-doux** has become **aigres-douces** to agree with the feminine plural word **pommes de terre**.

2.5 A word on pronunciation

The pronunciation of **vert** has been mentioned earlier. In some cases there is no change in pronunciation in the four forms of the adjective.

Example: bleu (m), bleue (f), bleus (mp) bleues   *(blue)*
noir (m), noire (f), noirs (m), noires (fp)   *(black)*

In other cases, the pronunciation will change when you add the **e** to make the feminine form.

Masculine		Feminine		
brun	⋯⟩	brune	⋯⟩	*brown*, pronunce the **ne**
grand	⋯⟩	grande	⋯⟩	*big*, pronunce the **de**
gris	⋯⟩	grise	⋯⟩	*grey*, pronouce the **se**
petit	⋯⟩	petite	⋯⟩	*small*, pronunce the **te**

2.6 Other ending patterns

We are going to divide these into five small groups. You should learn the ending patterns as well as the adjectives. You will come across others from each category but The main ones you will use from each group are included here.

1 Change er to ère

Masculine		Feminine		
cher	⋯⟩	chère	⋯⟩	*dear*
fier	⋯⟩	fière	⋯⟩	*proud*
premier	⋯⟩	première	⋯⟩	*first*
dernier	⋯⟩	dernière	⋯⟩	*last*
léger	⋯⟩	légère	⋯⟩	*light*

2 Change eux to euse/x to se

Masculine		Feminine		
brumeux	⋯⟩	brumeuse	⋯⟩	*misty/foggy*
dangereux	⋯⟩	dangereuse	⋯⟩	*dangerous*
furieux	⋯⟩	furieuse	⋯⟩	*furious*
heureux	⋯⟩	heureuse	⋯⟩	*happy*
jaloux	⋯⟩	jalouse	⋯⟩	*jealous*
nombreux	⋯⟩	nombreuse	⋯⟩	*numerous*
nuageux	⋯⟩	nuageuse	⋯⟩	*cloudy*
orageux	⋯⟩	orageuse	⋯⟩	*stormy*

3 Change if to ive

Masculine		Feminine		
actif	⋯⫸	active	⋯⫸	*active*
bref	⋯⫸	brève	⋯⫸	*brief*
négatif	⋯⫸	négative	⋯⫸	*negative*
positif	⋯⫸	positive	⋯⫸	*positive*
sportif	⋯⫸	sportive	⋯⫸	*sporty*
vif	⋯⫸	vive	⋯⫸	*lively*

4 Double the last letter and add e

Masculine		Feminine		
bas	⋯⫸	basse	⋯⫸	*low*
bon	⋯⫸	bonne	⋯⫸	*good*
gentil	⋯⫸	gentille	⋯⫸	*nice*
gros	⋯⫸	grosse	⋯⫸	*big/large*
moyen	⋯⫸	moyenne	⋯⫸	*average*
épais	⋯⫸	épaisse	⋯⫸	*thick*
gras	⋯⫸	grasse	⋯⫸	*fat/greasy (food)*

5 Adjectives that change completely

Masculine		Feminine		
* beau	⋯⫸	belle	⋯⫸	*handsome/beautiful*
blanc	⋯⫸	blanche	⋯⫸	*white*
doux	⋯⫸	douce	⋯⫸	*soft*
favori	⋯⫸	favorite	⋯⫸	*favourite*
faux	⋯⫸	fausse	⋯⫸	*false*
frais	⋯⫸	fraîche	⋯⫸	*fresh*
long	⋯⫸	longue	⋯⫸	*long*
* nouveau	⋯⫸	nouvelle	⋯⫸	*new*
public	⋯⫸	publique	⋯⫸	*public*
sec	⋯⫸	sèche	⋯⫸	*dry*
* vieux	⋯⫸	vieille	⋯⫸	*old*

2.7 Adjectives with two masculine forms

Remember that last fact mentioned on page 18? Well, this is it. There are only a few that have this form if the masculine noun begins with a vowel or silent **h**.

beau	becomes	**bel**
nouveau	becomes	**nouvel**
vieux	becomes	**vieil**

Example:
un bel oiseau	*a beautiful bird*
un nouvel étudiant	*a new student*
un vieil uniforme	*an old uniform*
un bel homme	*a handsome man*

These adjectives are also among those that come before the noun. For more on these, see *Position of adjectives* page 28.

The next exercises will focus on the previous topics.

Exercise 1

Choose the correct form of the adjective for the following exercises. Some of the words may not change:

1 La ville est (intéressant) _____.

2 J'ai les yeux (bleu) et les cheveux (noisette) _____.

3 Mon cartable est (lourd) _____.

4 J'ai besoin d'un crayon (rouge) _____.

5 Son père était (furieux) _____.

6 Elle est (heureux) _____.

7 Les montagnes sont (haut) _____.

8 Elles ont des amies (américain) _____.

9 Le lion est un (bel) _____ animal.

10 Ma couette est (blanc) _____.

Exercise 2

Look at these feminine adjectives. Match the opposites.

Example: courte ····> longue, *short* with *long*

blanche   dernière   forte

   haute   impolie   vieille

     noire

courte   paresseuse   nouvelle   chaude

  longue   positive   négative

     polie   basse

  première   nulle

     active   froide

En arrière !

Exercise 3

The adjectives above are in the feminine form. Now you have to pair at least ten of them with the correct masculine form. You should also give their English meaning. The first one is done for you as an example. The second one has been started!

	Masculine	·>	Feminine	·>	Meaning in English
1	court		courte		short
2	_____		blanche		_____
3	_____		_____		_____
4	_____		_____		_____
5	_____		_____		_____
6	_____		_____		_____
7	_____		_____		_____
8	_____		_____		_____
9	_____		_____		_____
10	_____		_____		_____

2.8 Position of adjectives

As already mentioned, most French adjectives are placed after the noun. The following adjectives are the ones that usually come before the noun. We have a nice way to remember them through the word **Bags**.

> **Bags**
>
> **B**eauty, all the adjectives have some connection with beauty, e.g. joli *(pretty)*
> **A**ge, e.g. **vieux** *(old)*
> **G**ood and Bad, e.g. **méchant** *(naughty)*
> **and**
> **S**ize, e.g. **vaste** *(huge)*

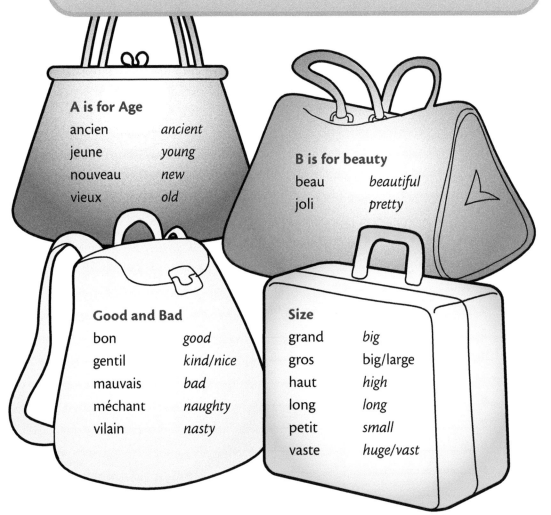

A is for Age

ancien	*ancient*
jeune	*young*
nouveau	*new*
vieux	*old*

B is for beauty

beau	*beautiful*
joli	*pretty*

Good and Bad

bon	*good*
gentil	*kind/nice*
mauvais	*bad*
méchant	*naughty*
vilain	*nasty*

Size

grand	*big*
gros	*big/large*
haut	*high*
long	*long*
petit	*small*
vaste	*huge/vast*

The other **A** that doesn't quite fit into these groups is **autre** *(other)*.

A couple of things you already do without thinking:

1 When you want to say **j'ai les cheveux longs** (*I have long hair*), the adjective comes after the noun.

2 Don't forget that numbers are classed as adjectives too.

> *Example:* **La deuxième rue à droite.** *The second road on the right.*
> **C'est la deuxième fois.** *It's the second time.*

Numbers will also come before the noun – something you probably do without thinking, when giving directions!

Exercise 4

Keeping in mind our bag idea, can you make at least five short descriptive phrases from the following selections? If you are not sure, remember to check if the noun is masculine or feminine, singular or plural.

NOUNS

une grande
des beaux
la méchante
des bonnes
un bon
un long
un vieux
un grand
un nouvel
un haut

jardin
château
bâtiment
trajet
repas
ami
nouvelles
cadeaux
fille
maison

Exercise 5

Choose a suitable adjective from the list of adjectives that come before the noun for the following sentences. Remember, the adjective must agree with the noun it describes.

1 Le _____ garçon s'appelle Shane.
2 J'adore les _____ vacances.
3 Cork est une_____ ville.
4 Meilleurs vœux pour le _____ An.
5 C'est une _____ journée.
6 Merci pour tes _____ cadeaux.
7 C'est ma _____ visite en Espagne.
8 J'ai un _____ frère et une _____ sœur.
9 Mon grand-père est un _____ homme.
10 Il y a des _____ fleurs dans le jardin.

2.9 Comparison of adjectives

Adjectives are used a lot to compare people, things, ideas, events, etc. In English, we usually add *er* to the adjective (small, smaller) or we place *more* or *less* in front of the adjective (more intelligent, less intelligent).

> **plus que** conveys the idea of *more than.*
> **moins que** conveys the idea of *less than.*
> **aussi que** conveys the idea of *as ... as.*

The adjective must agree in gender and number with the noun it is describing.

> *Example:*   Ciara est plus intelligente que son frère.
> *Ciara is more intelligent than her brother.*

We add an **e** after intelligent because the adjective is describing Ciara (a girl!).

Superlative is another word you hear associated with these types of adjectives. All it means is the idea of *the most*.

> *Example:*   Luke est le plus gentil.   *Luke is the nicest.*

You should remember that agreement is also needed here:

> *Example:*   Laura est la plus genti**lle**.   *Laura is the nicest.*

The superlative can also be used to really stress a point:

> *Example:*   Luke est le garçon le plus gentil de l'école.
> *Luke is the nicest boy in the school.*

After a superlative, the word *in* is translated by **de**.

Take a look at this conversation between Amy and Niamh as they discuss Alan and Mark.

Amy: Alan est plus intelligent que Mark.
Alan is more intelligent than Mark.

Niamh: Mais Mark est plus beau qu'Alan.
But Mark is more handsome/better looking than Alan.

Amy: Ah non ! Alan est le plus beau et il est le garçon le plus gentil de l'école aussi ! *Oh no! Alan is the most handsome and he is the nicest (most nice) boy in the school too.*

Que is shortened to **qu'** before a noun beginning with a vowel or a silent h, e.g. **qu'Alan**. Did you notice the use of the superlative in the last line?

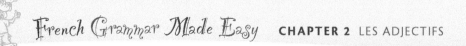
Exceptions to the rule

Bon, **petit** and **mauvais** do things their own way, taking a different form. Take a look:

> 1 When you want to say that something is good, better and best, you use these words;
>
> Bon/bonne *good*   meilleur(e) *better*   le/la meilleur(e) *best*
>
> 2 With the adjectives **mauvais** and **petit** you have two choices of forms:
>
> mauvais(e) *bad*   plus mauvais(e) *worse*   le/la pire *the worst*
> **or**
> mauvais(e) *bad*   plus mauvais(e) *worse*   le/la plus mauvais(e) *the worst*

mon ipod est petit

mon ipod est plus petit

mon ipod est le plus petit

> petit *small*   plus petit(e) *smaller*   le/la plus petit(e) *smallest*
> **or**
> petit(e) *small*   moindre *smaller*   le moindre/la moindre *smallest*

Don't forget we have this in English too with *better,* not *gooder*! Neither does *bad* become *badder.*

Exercise 6

Answer the following questions. In your answer, you need to replace the underlined word with the word in brackets. You should also decide if it would be more suitable to begin your answer with a **oui** (*yes*) or a **non** (*no*).

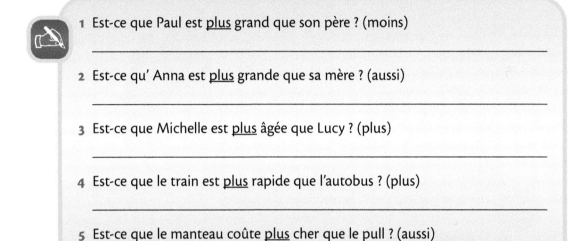

Example: Est-ce que Ben est *plus* grand que son frère ? (moins)

Non, Ben est moins grand que son frère.

1 Est-ce que Paul est <u>plus</u> grand que son père ? (moins)

_____

2 Est-ce qu' Anna est <u>plus</u> grande que sa mère ? (aussi)

_____

3 Est-ce que Michelle est <u>plus</u> âgée que Lucy ? (plus)

_____

4 Est-ce que le train est <u>plus</u> rapide que l'autobus ? (plus)

_____

5 Est-ce que le manteau coûte <u>plus</u> cher que le pull ? (aussi)

_____

Exercise 7

Answer the following questions using the names in brackets in your answer. Remember that the adjective must agree in gender and number with the noun it is describing.

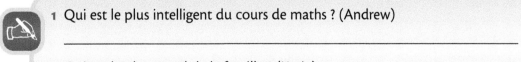

Example: Qui est le plus petit de la famille ? (Suzanne)

Suzanne est *la plus petite* de la famille.

1 Qui est le plus intelligent du cours de maths ? (Andrew)

_____

2 Qui est le plus grand de la famille ? (Katie)

_____

3 Qui est la plus belle du groupe ? (Sophie)

_____

4 Qui est le meilleur prof de l'école ? (M. Byrne)

_____

5 Qui sont les plus petits de la classe ? (Jessica et Lauren)

_____

Exercise 8

Alan and Mark are also talking, but not about the girls! They are far more concerned with who the best football player is.

 Fill in the gaps with **le meilleur, pire, bon**.

Mark: Ronaldo est _____ joueur du monde.
Fabregas est un _____ joueur aussi.

Alan: Et j'aime le stade de foot à Arsenal.

Mark: Moi aussi. Mais le stade
ici à l'école est le _____ !

2.10 Demonstrative adjectives

Demonstrative, demonstrate, show: can you see the break down? A demonstrative adjective simply shows or points out something. Again, it tells us more about the noun. In English, demonstrative adjectives appear as *this* or *that*, *these* or *those*. In French, because they are adjectives, the rule still applies. They agree in gender and number with the noun they describe. There are four forms: **ce**, **cet**, **cette** and **ces**.

> *note:*
> You will find it helpful to revise your vocabulary for clothes before doing the exercises in this section.

> **ce** is used before a masculine noun, **ce garçon** *(this boy)*.
>
> **cet** is used before a masculine noun beginning with a vowel, **cet arbre** *(this tree)*.
>
> **cette** is used before a feminine noun, **cette femme** *(this woman)*.
>
> **ces** is used before a noun in the plural, **ces livres** *(these books)*.

Exercise 9

Write the correct form of the demonstrative adjective in the following sentences.

> You may have learned the little rhyme **this, that, these and those, that's the way the th goes**. That's the rhyme you need to remember for demonstrative adjectives!

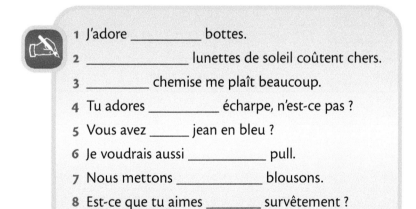

1 J'adore _____ bottes.

2 _____ lunettes de soleil coûtent chers.

3 _____ chemise me plaît beaucoup.

4 Tu adores _____ écharpe, n'est-ce pas ?

5 Vous avez _____ jean en bleu ?

6 Je voudrais aussi _____ pull.

7 Nous mettons _____ blousons.

8 Est-ce que tu aimes _____ survêtement ?

9 Ma sœur aime _____ talons.

10 Moi, je préfère _____ baskets.

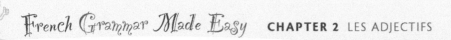
As sometimes you might be pointing out more than one thing, there is also a way around this to avoid confusion. In order to distinguish between them, we can add on **ci** and **là** to the demonstrative adjective. These are called suffixes. **Ci** indicates that the item is relatively near the speaker. **Là** suggests the item is further away. Let's take the example of a clothes shop.

You ask your friend what she thinks of a coat you are thinking of buying:

Qu'est-ce que tu penses de ce manteau-ci ?
What do you think of this coat?

She doesn't like it. Instead she tries to point you towards something else.

Ah non ! Je n'aime pas du tout cette couleur. Je préfère ce manteau-là.
Oh no! I don't like the colour at all. I prefer that coat.

Exercise 10

Write out a short conversation between you and your friend. You are in a clothes shop on a busy Saturday afternoon. Unfortunately your friend seems to be in a very bad humour and doesn't like any of the clothes you are picking out to try on and pointing out in the shop. Use the following vocabulary to help you.

Boîte de vocabulaire	
J'adore ce/cette/cet/ces …	*I love this …*
Qu'est-ce que tu penses de ?	*What do you think?*
La cabine d'essayage	*The changing room*
Ah non ! Ah oui !	*Oh no! Oh yes!*
C'est vraiment à la mode/démodé.	*It's really in fashion/old-fashioned.*
Tu n'as aucun goût !	*You have no taste!*

2.11 The interrogative adjective quel

Quel, meaning *which* and *what*, is also an adjective and must agree with the noun it refers to. Why is this an adjective, you ask? Well, take a look.

Quel blouson ? *Which jacket?*

Think back to our original definition. An adjective describes a noun or tells us more about a noun. *Which* is in this category too.

Remember you don't have to be a colour or a size to be an adjective!

Quel is for a masculine singular noun,	e.g. **Quel film ?** *Which film?*
Quelle is for a feminine singular noun,	e.g. **Quelle émission ?** *Which programme?*
Quels is for masculine plural nouns,	e.g. **Quels sports ?** *Which sports?*
Quelles is for feminine plural nouns,	e.g. **Quelles séries ?** *Which series?*

Quel is often used in expressions when it means *what a…*

Example: Quelle surprise !   *What a surprise!*
          Quel dommage !   *What a pity!*

Exercise 11
Use the correct form of quel in the following sentences.
Use your dictionary to help you.

1 _____ est la date aujourd'hui ?
2 _____ sport est-ce que tu aimes ?
3 _____ bonbons as-tu choisis ?
4 _____ livres ?
5 _____ beau garçon !
6 _____ belle fille !
7 _____ beau cadeau ! Merci beaucoup.
8 _____ âge as-tu ?
9 _____ langue est-ce qu'il parle ?
10 _____ sont tes passe-temps préférés ?

The adjective tout

Pronunciation: **tout** is pronounced like 'too' in English (the final 't' is silent). **Toute** and **toutes** are pronounced 'toot'.

Tout means *all, any, every*. It has four forms:

Tout for masculine singular, e.g. **tout enfant**, *every child*.

Toute for feminine singular, e.g. **toute ma famille**, *all my family*.

Tous for masculine plural, e.g. **tous mes amis**, *all my friends*.

Toutes for feminine plural, e.g. **toutes ces idées**, *all these ideas*.

Have you used the expression **tout le monde**? This means *everyone*, quite literally *all the world* (le monde, *the world*).

It always takes a verb in the third person singular.

Example: Tout le monde aime le chocolat. *Everyone likes chocolate.*

The expression **tous les jours** meaning *every day* is also really useful, as is **tout le temps**, *all the time*.

Exercise 12

Try the following exercise on **tout**. For most of the questions the clue is found in the question. For example, in question two, **la semaine** is feminine, so we need the feminine form of **tout**. If in doubt, get the dictionary out!

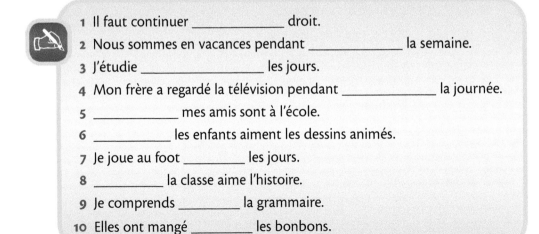

1 Il faut continuer _____ droit.

2 Nous sommes en vacances pendant _____ la semaine.

3 J'étudie _____ les jours.

4 Mon frère a regardé la télévision pendant _____ la journée.

5 _____ mes amis sont à l'école.

6 _____ les enfants aiment les dessins animés.

7 Je joue au foot _____ les jours.

8 _____ la classe aime l'histoire.

9 Je comprends _____ la grammaire.

10 Elles ont mangé _____ les bonbons.

2.13 The possessive adjective

Mon, **ma**, **mes**, **ton**, **ta**, **tes**, **son**, **sa**, **ses** are possessive adjectives because they tell us who owns something. They also tell us more about a noun. We would use them instead of **un**, **une**, **des**, **le**, **la**, **les** to indicate to whom something belongs. In your textbook, you have probably used them with family members to indicate **mon père** *(my dad)*, **ton oncle** *(your uncle)*, etc. The key thing you need to remember here is that:

> **It is the gender of the object that is owned which matters, not the owner.**

You need to learn these adjectives off by heart, but it's easy! There's a good little rhythm to them, particularly when you say them downwards, e.g., **mon**, **ma**, **mes**, **ton**, **ta**, **tes**.

	my	your	his/her	our	your	their
Masculine	mon	ton	son	notre	votre	leur
Feminine	ma	ta	sa	notre	votre	leur
Plural	mes	tes	ses	nos	vos	leurs

A quick word on leur

Here, **leur(s)** means *their*. It is a possessive adjective and takes an **s** when the object it is describing is plural. **Leur livre** is simply *their book*, but **leurs livres** means *their books*. Like in English, *their* is the plural word for *his, her, its*. **Son, sa, ses** become **leur** in the plural.

Leur can also be a personal pronoun. Please see the chapter on pronouns for more detail on this.

It is very important to remember that it is the gender of the object that matters and not the gender of the subject. Let's take the example of the word *watch*, which is feminine in French, **la montre**. If I am a girl and it is my watch, it is **ma montre**. If I am a boy who owns the watch, it is still **ma montre**.

Son, **sa** and **ses** can mean *his, her* or *its*, depending on the context, or the situation described. Let's look at this using the example of **lit**, a masculine word meaning *bed*. **Son lit** can mean *his bed, her bed* or *its bed*. You might be talking about your dog's bed. Others, who consider their dog a human, might translate it into English as *his* or *her* bed! Again, it is all about how we understand the given situation. The word *context* is really important to your understanding of this. Take a look at this short passage describing Paul's first day in secondary school.

Exercise 13

Son professeur d'anglais s'appelle Monsieur Thomas. Paul est nerveux.
La classe commence à 10h. Il y a vingt-deux élèves dans sa classe.
Il cherche ses crayons dans sa trousse.

From this short passage, answer the following three questions:

1 In the first sentence, what does the possessive adjective **son** stand for?

   _____

2 What does the possessive adjective **sa** stand for in the fourth sentence?

   _____

3 Can you translate the last sentence, paying particular attention to the possessive adjectives?

   _____

Checklist:

- Did you understand what **son, sa** and **ses** stood for?
- Did you remember that what matters is the gender of the word and not the person involved? You knew from the context that the last sentence would be translated as *he looks for his pencils in his pencil case.*
- If you were talking about Colette's first day at school, you only have to change the word Paul to Colette.

  True ☐   False ☐   Please tick

When describing two or more nouns, a possessive adjective must be used in front of each one:

Example: Mon frère et ma sœur. *My brother and my sister.*

In French, the possessive adjectives are not used for body parts. The **article défini** is used so **je me brosse les dents** means *I brush my teeth.*

Liaison

Do not forget to make the liaison between the plural forms of the possessive adjectives and words that begin with a vowel sound. **Ma**, **ta** and **sa** become **mon**, **ton** and **son** before feminine nouns beginning with a vowel.

Example: mon école, son amie.

Exercise 14

Give the correct possessive adjective for the following sentences:

Jack is introducing his family to his friends Conor and Sinéad. There are quite a lot of people in the room. Fill in the correct part of the possessive adjective:

Jack présente sa famille.

Voici ____*ma*____ sœur Kate et _____ frère Matt, et _____ parents. Voici _____ autre sœur Susan et _____ enfants, et _____ chien, Skip. _____ famille est assez grande !

Jack introduces his friends to everyone:

Voilà Conor et Sinéad, _____ amis.

Exercise 15

Using **mon**, **ma** or **mes**, name the items in this chef's kitchen.

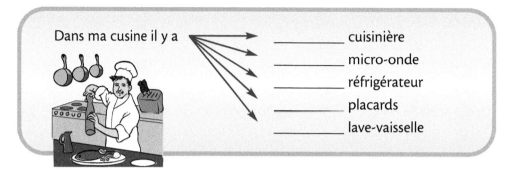

Dans ma cusine il y a

_____ cuisinière

_____ micro-onde

_____ réfrigérateur

_____ placards

_____ lave-vaisselle

Exercise 16

Using **son**, **sa** or **ses**, name the items in Hervé's room.

Dans sa chambre il y a

_____ lit

_____ posters

_____ ordinateur

_____ lecteur CD

_____ table de chevet

_____ télévision

Exercise 17

Fill in the gaps below with either **notre** or **nos**, **votre** or **vos**, **leur** or **leurs**.
(You should revise your vocabulary on sport to make good use of the exercise.)

1 Nous avons _____ raquettes.

2 Ils ont _____ entraînement le samedi.

3 _____ amis sortent avec vous ?

4 Nous supportons _____ équipe de foot.

5 Ils portent _____ baskets.

6 Vous devez porter _____ casque.

You may be taking a few sections at a time for this chapter and that's perfectly ok.
Check what applies to what you have been working on and tick off accordingly.
You will be very impressed with yourself when you can tick off all categories,
so keep up the good work!

Récapitulez

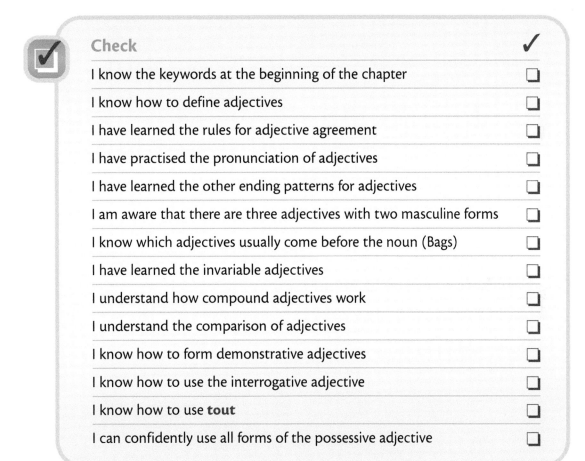

Check	✔
I know the keywords at the beginning of the chapter	❑
I know how to define adjectives	❑
I have learned the rules for adjective agreement	❑
I have practised the pronunciation of adjectives	❑
I have learned the other ending patterns for adjectives	❑
I am aware that there are three adjectives with two masculine forms	❑
I know which adjectives usually come before the noun (Bags)	❑
I have learned the invariable adjectives	❑
I understand how compound adjectives work	❑
I understand the comparison of adjectives	❑
I know how to form demonstrative adjectives	❑
I know how to use the interrogative adjective	❑
I know how to use **tout**	❑
I can confidently use all forms of the possessive adjective	❑

Chapter 3
Le Présent de l'indicatif
The Present Tense

Key words

- Présent de l'indicatif
- Infinitive
- Verb conjugation
- Verb groups
- Pronouns, personal and reflexive

- Irregular verbs
- Reflexive verbs
- Use of pouvoir, vouloir and devoir
- Use of French pronoun on
- Imperative

3.1 A quick word before we begin

In English there are two forms of the present tense:

I give, I am giving.

In French, there is only one form,

le présent de l'indicatif.

You need to know this term.

So, **je donne** means *I give* **or** *I am giving*. It can also mean *I do give*. **Je donne** is used for all two English meanings.

There are three main groups of regular verbs in French.

- the **-er** family
- the **-ir** family
- the **-re** family

Two other groups are the *reflexive verbs* and the *irregular group*.

The infinitive is the full name of the verb, like **parler**, **finir**, **attendre**.

1 To get the present tense of a regular verb, firstly, we go to the infinitive of the verb. This is the form of the verb you find in the dictionary. It is the verb before it is broken down.

2 Take away the **-er**, **-ir** and **-re** endings and you are left with the *stem*.

Infinitive		Stem
Par**ler**	⋯⋗	parl
Fin**ir**	⋯⋗	fin
Atten**dre**	⋯⋗	attend

3 Now we add the present tense endings to the stem. We call this process *verb conjugation*.

3.2 Group 1: -er verbs

Rappel !

Donner is the verb *to give*. This is the infinitive of the verb. In other words it is the verb before it is broken down and given its proper endings.

Example: **Donner** – *to give*

Je donn**e**	Nous donn**ons**
Tu donn**es**	Vous donn**ez**
Il/Elle donn**e**	Ils/Elles donn**ent**

Rappel !

Pronunciation: Don't pronounce the **ent** part of the verb in the **ils/elles** form, or the **s** in the **tu** form!

Remember the **vous** form is used for *you* plural in English and also to show respect.

Exercise 1
Les verbes en -er au présent

Write the correct form of the verb in the present tense into your copy.

> 1 Je (porter) _____ des chaussures.
>
> 2 Il (tomber) _____ toujours.
>
> 3 Nous (visiter) _____ l'Aquadome à Tralee.
>
> 4 Elle (aimer) _____ sa famille.
>
> 5 Ils (passer) _____ une semaine chez ses grands-parents.
>
> 6 Alan (habiter) _____ à Donegal.
>
> 7 Les filles (chanter) _____ très bien.
>
> 8 Sophie et ses amies (passer) _____ une semaine en France.
>
> 9 Vous (louer) _____ une caravane à Nice ?
>
> 10 Ma mère et ma tante (dîner) _____ au restaurant.

3.3 Group 2: -ir verbs

> *Example:* **Finir** – *to finish*

All the **sssss** here!

> Again *don't pronounce* the nt.
> **Ils finissent** will sound like the name Denise in English!

Finir	
Je fin**is**	Nous fin**issons**
Tu fin**is**	Vous fin**issez**
Il/Elle fin**it**	Ils/Elles fin**issent**

Exercise 2
Les verbes en **-ir** au présent

Write the correct form of the verb in the present tense into your copy.

1 Je (choisir) _____ un cadeau pour mon frère.
2 Il (remplir) _____ son verre jusqu'au bord.
3 Sophie et Susan (rougir) _____ toujours.
4 Je (saisir) _____ l'occasion pour me présenter.
5 Orla (obéir) à ses parents et elle (manger) _____ ses légumes.
6 Mon grand-père (vieillir) _____.
7 Ils (bâtir) _____ les maisons.
8 Mes petites sœurs (grandir) _____.
9 Paul (choisir) _____ la meilleure voiture.
10 Áine (réfléchir) _____ beaucoup.

3.4 Group 3: **-re** verbs

Example: **Vendre**

Pronunciation: Only pronounce the **d** in the plural forms as it is followed directly by a vowel, **o/e**. For the singular forms, the **d** is silent.

s/s/-/ons/ez/ent are the endings here

Je vend**s**	Nous vend**ons**
Tu vend**s**	Vous vend**ez**
Il/Elle vend	Ils/Elles vend**ent**

Exercise 3
Les verbes en -re au présent

Write the correct form of the verb in the present tense.

1 Je (tondre) _____ la pelouse chaque samedi.

2 Ils (perdre) _____ leurs livres tout le temps.

3 Le boucher (vendre) _____ de la viande.

4 Les enfants (attendre) _____ leur repas.

5 Le prof (descendre) _____ l'escalier.

6 Elle (attendre) _____ l'autobus.

7 Le suspect (répondre) _____ aux questions.

8 Tu (entendre) _____ des bruits dans le jardin.

9 Je (perdre) _____ toujours quelque chose.

10 Attention au chien ! Il (mordre) _____.

3.5 Subject pronouns

Je, **tu**, **il**, **elle**, **nous**, **vous**, **ils** and **elles** are pronouns. As there are several types of pronouns, to further define them we call these ones *personal pronouns*, meaning simply that they take the place of a person's name.

If we want to say a person's name, _____

Example: Marc instead of **il** *(he)*,

To say *Marc gives*, simply use the same verb ending as we would use for **il**, i.e. **Marc donne**.

Let's study the grid below to see this more fully worked out.

We will use the verb **choisir** (*to choose*):

Pronoun (Taking the place of someone's name)		Noun	Verb – Choisir
Je	*I*	Your name (*this is called the 1st person singular*)	choisis
Tu	*You*	Your friend's name (*you guessed it! 2nd person singular*)	choisis
Il	*He*	Paul (*3rd person singular*)	choisit
Elle	*She*	Sinéad (*3rd person singular*)	choisit
Nous	*We*	Ray and I (*Careful! 1st person plural*)	choisissons
Vous *You* (*more than one person or to show respect*)		Nicole and Luke/Your teacher (*2nd person plural*)	choisissez
Ils *They* (*masculine or a group of males and females*)		Nick and James (*3rd person plural*)	choisissent
Elles *They* (*female*)		Ciara and Niamh (*3rd person plural*)	choisissent

3.6 **Group 4: Reflexive verbs**

Shhhhh!

We call these **les verbes pronominaux** in French.

A hint with this group of verbs is that it is mainly made up of **-er** verbs with an extra pronoun attached. We call this a **reflexive pronoun** and it can be found between the personal pronoun and the verb. The reflexive pronoun refers back to the person or thing which is the subject of the verb (myself, yourself, ourselves, etc.) Try to remember that these reflexive verbs have three parts.

Reflexive verbs are verbs which either:

1 Reflect the action back onto the subject

> *Example:* **Je me lave.** *I wash myself.*

or

2 Have the sense of *each other.*

> *Example:* **Ils se disputent.** *They fight with each other.*

Using the idea of three columns is helpful.

> *Example:* **se reposer** – *to relax*

personal pronoun	reflective pronoun	verb
Je	me	repose
Tu	te	reposes
Il	se	repose
Elle	se	repose
Nous	nous	reposons
Vous	vous	reposez
Ils /Elles	se	reposent

So remember, you must have three columns in 'building' up a reflexive verb in the present tense; otherwise it won't be built properly!

Other examples of reflexive verbs are **se promener**, **se coucher**, **se réveiller**, **se demander**. When the verb begins with *a vowel* or a *h* as in **s'amuser** or **s'habiller**, the **me** shortens to **m**, the **te** shortens to **t** and the **se** shortens to **s**.

> *Example:*   **Je m'amuse.**

Note:
Remember, when you look these up in the dictionary, they will have the word **se** before them.

Exercise 4
Test Yourself!

Look up the verbs **s'amuser**, **s'habiller** and **se demander** in your dictionary. Write down the meanings in your copy.

Exercise 5
Now write out the present tense of each of these verbs in full. Don't forget that you need the three columns to build your structure properly.

Exercise 6
Here is Nadine's description of her morning. Can you fill in the missing parts of the verb? Remember to change the **se** to **me**!

> *Example:*   Je (se réveiller)   ····▷   Je me réveille.

Je (se réveiller) _____ à sept heures.

Je (se lever) _____ à sept heures et demie.

Je (se laver) _____ dans la salle de bains.

Je (se brosser) _____ les dents.

Je (s'habiller) _____ dans la chambre.

Exercise 7

Can you change the **je** form in Exercise 6 to **nous**?
What will the reflexive pronoun be this time?

Exercise 8

Write out these reflexive verbs in the present tense.

> *Example:*   Je (se disputer) avec mon frère.
>
> Je me dispute avec mon frère.

1 Je (se coucher) _____ tard le soir.

2 Tu (se réveiller) _____ tôt ?

3 Nous (se laver) _____ très vite.

4 Les enfants (se brosser) _____ les dents.

5 Ils (s'amuser) _____ bien en ville.

6 Les filles (se maquiller) _____ quand elles sortent.

7 Vous (se baigner) _____ ?

8 Anna et Stephen (se dépêcher) _____ pour ne pas rater le train.

9 Mes amis (se disputer) _____ avec leurs parents.

10 Ma cousine (se marier) _____ demain.

> *Note:*
> Keep in mind the need for three parts to the verb and don't forget to change the 'se' to agree with the personal pronoun
> (**je** with **me**, **tu** with **te**, etc.).

3.7 **Group 5: Irregular verbs**

– some are a little irregular and some are a lot!

We call these *irregular verbs* because they don't quite follow the rules.
Some only have tiny changes and others have more.

1 A little irregular!

Learn these verbs **par cœur** !

Verbs ending in **-ger**

Other **-ger** verbs you may come across are:

- **loger** to lodge,
- **ranger** to put away,
- **plonger**, to dive.

The **nous** form stresses the **ge**, mangeons

Nager *to swim*	**manger** *to eat*	**voyager** *to travel*
je nage	Je mange	je voyage
tu nages	tu manges	tu voyages
il/elle nage	il/elle mange	il/elle voyage
nous nageons	nous mangeons	nous voyageons
vous nagez	vous mangez	vous voyagez
ils/elles nagent	ils/elles mangent	ils/elles voyagent

For verbs ending in **-ger**, the **e** is kept in for the **nous** form to keep the **g** sound soft.

2 Note the accents here!

acheter *to buy*	**se promener** *to go for a walk*
j'achète	je me promène
tu achètes	tu te promènes
il/elle achète	il/elle se promène
nous achetons	nous nous promenons
vous achetez	vous vous promenez
ils/elles achètent	ils/elles se promènent

> No accent for the **nous** and **vous** forms

Study these verbs carefully and learn which part takes the *grave (è)* and which takes the *aigu (é)*. There are accents on all parts but the **nous** and **vous** forms are different.

Espérer *to hope for*	**Préférer** *to prefer*
j'espère	je préfère
tu espères	tu préfères
il/elle espère	il/elle préfère
nous espérons	nous préférons
vous espérez	vous préférez
ils/elles espèrent	ils/elles préfèrent

> See how the accent changes for the **nous** and **vous** forms

3 Verbs ending in **-cer** and **-yer**

Placer *to place* is the one you will come across most often. In the **nous** form we change the **c** to **ç** to keep a soft sound. If not it would sound like the word **plaque**, which builds up on your teeth ! **Commencer** *to start*, **lancer** *to throw*, **prononcer** *to pronounce* and **remplacer** *to replace* also take this change.

je place	nous plaçons
tu places	vous placez
il/elle place	ils/elles placent

Here we change the **y** to **i** in all forms except the **nous** and **vous**. **Envoyer** *to send* is the one you will come across most often but **employer** *to employ* and **nettoyer** *to clean* are also common.

Envoyer *to send*	
j'envoie	nous envoyons
tu envoies	vous envoyez
il/elle envoie	ils/elles envoient

> A **y** is used instead of **i** in the **nous** and **vous** forms.

4 A lot! Keep at it. Learn them now, this once, and then the pressure will be off.

aller *to go*	**avoir** *to have*	**être** *to be*	**faire** *to do*
je vais	j'ai	je suis	je fais
tu vas	tu as	tu es	tu fais
il/elle va	il/elle a	il/elle est	il/elle fait
nous allons	nous avons	nous sommes	nous faisons
vous allez	vous avez	vous êtes	vous faites
ils/elles vont	ils/elles ont	ils/elles sont	ils/elles font

> ... vont ...
> ... ont ...
> ... sont ...

> Note that the **ils/elles** parts of these four verbs end in **ont**, instead of the usual **ent**!

See the similarities here? It's really useful to remember the **ils** and **elles** form this way, but don't mix them up. You should also be careful of the spelling of **vous êtes**.

partir *to leave*	prendre *to take*	sortir *to go out*
je pars	je prends	je sors
tu pars	tu prends	tu sors
il/elle part	il/elle prend	il/elle sort
nous partons	nous prenons	nous sortons
vous partez	vous prenez	vous sortez
il/elles partent	ils/elles prennent	il/elles sortent

Exercise 9

Fill in the gaps in the postcard: (All five groups of verbs are included, so **attention !**)

Nice, le 9 juin

Salut Nicole !

Me voici à Nice. Il (faire) _____ du soleil. Je (s'amuser) _____ beaucoup.

Je (nager) _____, je (faire) _____ de la voile et je (aller) _____ en ville tous les jours.

J'(adorer) _____ la cuisine française. Le soir nous (faire) _____ des barbecues ou (manger) _____ dans les restaurants du quartier.

Nous (partir) _____ dans deux semaines. Comment (aller) _____ toute la famille ?

À bientôt,

Claire

Nicole Martin,
99, rue La Fontaine
35000 Rennes

Exercise 10
Can you write a similar postcard using some of the verbs you have learned?
Of course you can!

Choose a holiday destination in Ireland and write a postcard to your penpal,
Luc, who lives in Lille in France.

Tell him that:

> you are enjoying yourself
> it is a bit cold
> you eat in nice restaurants
> you like the shops

Exercise 11
Write the appropriate form of the verb from the **mélange** of verbs below.

Jouer	Je	*joue*	Tu	_____	Ils	_____
Choisir	Tu	_____	Il	_____	Nous	_____
Faire	Elle	_____	Ils	_____	Vous	_____
Vendre	Il	_____	Nous	_____	Elles	_____
Aller	Je	_____	Vous	_____	Elle	_____
Avoir	Il	_____	Je	_____	Tu	_____
Être	Je	_____	Tu	_____	Vous	_____
Descendre	Ils	_____	Elle	_____	Je	_____

Exercise 12
Mots Cachés !

Can you find the infinitive for these verbs? Once you have worked them out, your next task is to find them in the wordsearch.

To go _____	To have _____
To make/do _____	To choose _____
To eat _____	To finish _____
To play _____	To sell _____
To swim _____	To travel _____

e	s	l	f	d	v	e	r	x	r	m	v	n	e	r
r	f	y	n	a	d	j	j	i	q	i	a	g	e	o
d	d	g	y	m	i	v	o	z	s	g	n	g	p	d
n	a	l	l	e	r	r	u	b	e	i	n	i	y	s
e	r	i	o	v	a	x	e	r	a	a	o	w	f	d
v	m	r	o	x	n	r	r	m	m	w	d	h	z	p
q	v	f	g	y	x	v	z	h	u	z	k	j	c	q
r	e	g	a	y	o	v	i	u	j	o	c	k	e	m
n	n	t	y	o	l	e	n	r	t	i	y	c	a	l
e	z	o	j	b	k	l	q	v	x	z	e	b	v	e

3.8 Pouvoir/Vouloir/Devoir

These are irregular verbs in French that we are going to zoom in on a little closer. They are known as auxiliary verbs or helping verbs because they help another verb to form the sentence correctly.

Remember the building we talked about in relation to reflexive verbs? Well, these are like the foundations of a building. Without these, we couldn't build the rest of the sentence correctly.

Je dois	Je peux	Je veux
Tu dois	Tu peux	Tu veux
Il/Elle doit	Il/Elle peut	Il/Elle veut
Nous devons	Nous pouvons	Nous voulons
Vous devez	Vous pouvez	Vous voulez
Ils/ Elles doivent	Ils/Elles peuvent	Ils/ Elles veulent

Study some examples to see how they work:

Elle doit travailler.	*She has to work.*
Je veux regarder le match.	*I want to watch the match.*
Elles peuvent faire leurs devoirs maintenant.	*They can do their homework now.*

Exercise 13

Choose the correct part of the verb to make the sentences below read correctly.
Can you say what the sentences mean in English?

1 J'ai soif. Je *veux/doit/veut/peut* un verre d'eau, s'il vous plaît.

2 Simone *veux/veut/voulons* skier mais elle ne *peut/peux/devons* pas.

3 Vous avez mal à la gorge. Vous *doit/devez/peux* rester au lit.

4 Nous avons un exam. Nous *doivent/dois/devons* étudier.

5 Nous n'aimons pas les magasins. Nous ne *voulons/veulent/peuvent* pas aller en ville.

6 Elle *veut/veux/veulent* voir le film.

7 Ils *doivent/devons/doit* étudier ce soir.

8 Je *dois/doit/doivent* partir.

9 Nous *voulons/veulent/veux* manger au restaurant.

10 Jean et Luc *veulent/veux/voulons* partir demain.

3.9 The use of the French pronoun on

(More about this in the chapter on pronouns) What is so important or useful about this little word, you may ask? Well, it has several uses.

1 It is very commonly used in spoken French.

2 The third person singular of the verb is used with **on**. In other words, it will have the same verb endings as the **il** and **elle** form.

3 It can mean *someone/you/they/we* and *one*.

Example:	On joue aux boules en France.
One possible meaning:	*We play boules in France.*
Another possible meaning:	*In France, one plays boules, giving the idea that boules are played, that people in general play boules.*

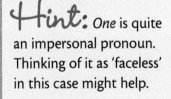

Hint: *One* is quite an impersonal pronoun. Thinking of it as 'faceless' in this case might help.

Depending on the context of what you are reading or writing about, the meaning would be clear. Always keep in mind that **on** has the same ending as **il** and **elle**.

Exercise 14

Paying particular attention to **on**, can you say what the following sentences mean?

1 On va à la piscine.

2 On joue au foot à l'école.

3 On se couche tard pendant les vacances.

4 On frappe à la porte.

5 On peut sortir quand on est chez ma tante.

6 On mange des cuisses de grenouilles en France.

7 On joue au hurling en Irlande.

8 On peut manger des frites de temps en temps.

9 En Allemagne, on boit de la bière.

10 En Écosse, on joue au rugby.

3.10 The Imperative

When you give someone directions, make a request or order someone to do something, you use the imperative.

... tournez à droite ...

To form the imperative, you use the 2nd person singular, 1st person plural and 2nd person plural of the present tense, the **tu**, **nous** and **vous** form.

So, how do I form the **impératif**?

It's easy, honestly!

You use the present tense of the verb concerned, but leave out the pronouns **tu**, **nous** and **vous**.

There is just one small thing to point out here.
For **-er** verbs, you take away the final **s** from the **tu** form:

Parle

Look at these examples:

- This is the **tu** form of **parler** in the imperative: **Parle** ! *Talk!*
- The **tu** form of the imperative is used with people you know well.
- The **nous** form: **Parlons** ! *Let's talk!* The **nous** form is to suggest the idea of *let's*.

And the **vous** form: **Parlez** ! *Talk!*
The **vous** form is used with more than one person or with someone you don't know well.

Note:
Don't forget to include an exclamation mark every time you use the imperative!

-ir and **-re** verbs

	-ir	-re
(tu)	choisis	attends
(nous)	choisissons	attendons
(vous)	choisissez	attendez

Remember to leave out the pronouns **tu**, **nous** and **vous** for the imperatif.

To make a sentence negative in **l'impératif**:

Use **ne** and **pas** if you want to tell someone not to do something.

Example: **Ne** mange **pas** trop ! *Don't eat too much!*

Exercise 15

Using the imperative, give the correct form of the verb in brackets.

1 (Tourner) à droite, Paul !

2 Amy, (travailler) !

3 (Apporter) vos maillots de bain à la piscine !

4 Barry et John, (fermer) les fenêtres !

5 (Sortir) ensemble ce soir !

6 Ne (vendre) pas la voiture Papa !

7 N'(oublier) pas tes livres !

8 Niamh, ne (manger) pas trop !

9 (Jouer) au tennis !

10 Dean et Michelle, (réponder) à toutes les questions !

3.11 The Present Participle

Explain please!

We also have this in English. It ends in *-ing*: *selling, giving, looking*.
In French it ends in **-ant**: **vendant**, **donnant**, **regardant**.
So remember, the **-ant** is equal to the *-ing*.

Formation of present participle / le participe présent
To form the present participle:

1 Take the **nous** form of the present tense.

> *Example:*   nous vendons

2 Now drop the **-ons** and add **-ant**.

> *Example:*   nous vendons   ⋯⋙   vend**ons**   ⋯⋙   vend**ant**

Remember, the **nous** form of irregular verbs in the present will follow the same rules.

> *Example:*   nous faisons   ⋯⋙   faisons   ⋯⋙   fais**ant**

There are only three exceptions to the rule. Take a look:

Être ⋯⋗ this is **nous sommes** ⋯⋗ but the stem now becomes ⋯⋗ **ét**
now add on **ant** ⋯⋗ and voilà! ⋯⋗ **Étant**, or *being* in English

Avoir ⋯⋗ **nous avons** ⋯⋗ **Ayant** or *having* in English

Savoir ⋯⋗ **nous savons** ⋯⋗ **sachant** or *knowing* in English

The while, on, by doing something theory:

The **participe présent** is really useful when used with the preposition **en** to convey the following ideas:

On/upon doing something

En arrivant au musée, elle a vu les peintures.
On arriving at the museum, she saw the paintings.

While doing something

Luke s'est cassé la jambe en descendant l'escalier.
Luke broke his leg while walking down the stairs.

By doing something

En faisant les devoirs, les élèves peuvent réussir à l'école.
By doing homework, pupils can succeed in school.

The present participle is used to link two actions happening at the same time:

This links two simultaneous actions!

Exercise 16

Now insert the correct form of the verb to show the **participe présent** in action:

1 Je mange mon petit déjeuner (while chatting) _____ avec ma famille.

2 Mon frère fait ses devoirs (while watching) _____ la télé.

3 Alex gagne son argent de poche (by doing) _____ le ménage.

4 (On/Upon arriving) _____ à l'école, nous allons à la cantine.

5 (On leaving) _____ la gare, les touristes vont à l'office de tourisme.

6 (By going) _____ en vacances, je suis fauchée.

7 (While waiting for) _____ le train, j'ai écouté mon iPod.

8 (While doing) _____ la vaisselle, j'ai cassé une tasse.

9 Je me suis fait mal au dos (by carrying) _____ les valises.

10 J'ai vu un accident de voiture (on/upon coming out) _____ du magasin.

Exercise 17

Your final task in this chapter is to put all you have learned into practice.
Compose a letter that you are going to send by e-mail to your correspondant
Christophe who lives in Paris. Include at least five of the following points:

You should:

- Say that you are his new penpal.

- Tell him your name and your age.

- Say where you live and where it is in Ireland.

- Talk about your family.

- Describe your school.

- Give him a brief description of your house.

- Tell him your favourite subjects in school.

- Briefly describe your routine in the morning.

- Talk about your hobbies and what you like to do at the weekend.

- Ask him about what he likes to do in his free time.

- Ask him to write soon. (*Did you notice? You have been using the imperative here all along!*)

Now that you have completed this chapter, can you complete the following checklist? Now, let's finish with a look back on what you should know.

Récapitulez

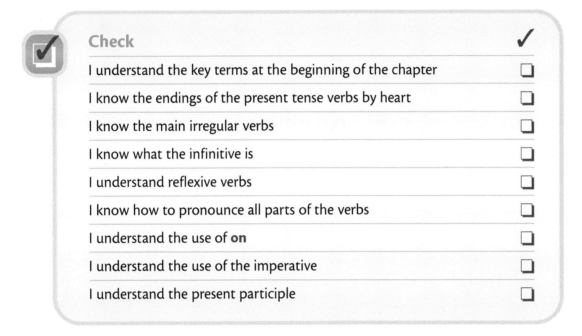

Check	✓
I understand the key terms at the beginning of the chapter	☐
I know the endings of the present tense verbs by heart	☐
I know the main irregular verbs	☐
I know what the infinitive is	☐
I understand reflexive verbs	☐
I know how to pronounce all parts of the verbs	☐
I understand the use of **on**	☐
I understand the use of the imperative	☐
I understand the present participle	☐

Chapter 4
Les Prépositions
Prepositions

Key words

···⟫ Relationship
···⟫ Franglais
···⟫ Idiomatic phrases

4.1 A quick word

It's all about the small words here. Let's start with a definition of prepositions:

> **They are the little words that relate nouns and pronouns in a sentence.**

> *Example:* We live **in** Kildare. My cousins live **near** us. I'm talking **to** Ann.
> The present is **for** you. Like conjunctions, you have probably
> used some of these already in French without really noticing them.

> *Example:* J'habite **à** Kildare.
> *I live in Kildare.*
> _____
> Or what about   Mes livres sont **sur** la table.
> *My books are on the table.*

In this chapter, we will look at the prepositions you are probably using already.
We will also look at **à** (meaning *to* or *at*) and **de** (meaning *of* or *from*).

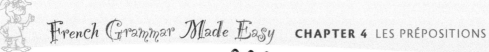
I'm also going to give you a vocabulary checklist here before we begin.

> You will find the exercises in this chapter much easier if you revise the following:
>
> ☐   The buildings in your town
> ☐   Sports/hobbies
> ☐   Animals/pets
> ☐   Your classroom
> ☐   Your house

4.2   Really useful prepositions you may be using already

The following prepositions are really useful. I will divide them into groups according to how you are using them.

Group 1
To show where an object is:

dans	*in*
Je suis *dans* le salon.	*I am in the sitting room.*
derrière	*behind*
La poubelle est *derrière* la porte.	*The bin is behind the door.*
devant	*in front of*
Le bureau est *devant* la porte.	*The desk is in front of the door.*
entre	*between*
Joe est *entre* Tony et Niamh.	*Joe is between Tony and Niamh.*
sur	*on*
Le livre est *sur* le bureau.	*The book is on the desk.*
sous	*under*
Mon sac est *sous* la chaise.	*My bag is under the chair.*

Group 2
To indicate location of a shop/building:

> Remember your rules for **de** here:
> **de+le** becomes **du**; près **du** bureau,
> **de+les** becomes **des**; en face **des** magasins.

au bout de	*at the end of*
L'église est *au bout de* la rue.	*The church is at the end of the street.*
au coin de	*on the corner of*
Le boucherie est *au coin de* la place.	*The butcher's is on the corner of the square.*
à côté de	*beside*
Ma maison est *à côté de* la plage.	*My house is beside the beach.*
aux environs de	*on the outskirts of*
Ma famille habite *aux environs de* Dublin.	*My family live on the outskirts of Dublin.*
en face de	*opposite*
La poste est *en face du* café.	*The post office is opposite the café.*
le long de	*the length of*
Les filles se promènent *le long du* parc.	*The girls walk the length of the park.*
près de	*near*
La poste est *près de* la banque.	*The post office is near the bank.*
au bord de la mer/du lac/de la rivière	*by the sea/lake/river*
Le camping se trouve *au bord de la mer*.	*The campsite is by the sea.*

Group 3
A few others that you might use here and there:

après	*after*
Je vais faire mes devoirs *après* les cours.	*I am going to do my homework after the class.*
avant	*before*
Je vais arriver *avant* midi.	*I am going to arrive before midday.*
avec	*with*
J'irai *avec* mes parents.	*I will go with my parents.*
sans	*without*
Il est parti *sans* son portefeuille.	*He left without his wallet.*
vers	*around/towards*
Nous partons *vers* 14h30.	*We are leaving around 2.30pm.*

Now, let's put them into practice!

Exercise 1

Use a suitable preposition from the lists on pages 70–71 in the following sentences.
Your aim here is to use a different preposition each time.

1 Ma sœur travaille au magasin _____ chez moi.

2 La mairie est _____ l'église.

3 J'ai beaucoup de posters _____ les murs de
   ma chambre.

4 La souris est _____
   le chat et le chien.

5 Les fleurs sont _____ le vase.

6 Il y a un jardin _____ et _____
   la maison.

7 Suzanne est assise _____ Marie.

8 Le week-end je sors _____ mes amis.

9 Mes livres sont _____ ma table.

10 Notre maison se trouve _____ la rue.

Exercise 2

1 Write a short paragraph describing your bedroom, paying particular attention to the location of objects.

2 Now write 3–5 sentences describing the location of buildings in your town or village. (Three if it is a small village, five if it is a big town!)

Exercise 3

Alan and Amy are going on a date. Everything is going wrong, however.

1 Write Alan's text to Amy in French. He says he is opposite the cinema, in the café on the corner with his friends.

2 Amy is horrified! She is not going to go into the café by herself to meet all his friends. Write her text to Alan in French, she is at the end of the street, near the park. Hmmph!

4.3 À, meaning to or at

We've already said that prepositions are small, but this one is tiny. Yes, small in size, but big in importance. It is the preposition **à**. When you start learning French, you learn about how **à** is used before the name of a town.

J'habite *à* Dublin. *I live in Dublin.*	⋯⇨ In English, we translate the **à** as *in* because
Il habite *à* Limerick. *He lives in Limerick.*	obviously it makes more sense this way.
Nous allons *à* Galway pour nos vacances.	⋯⇨ Here we would translate the **à** as *to*.
We are going to Galway for our holidays.	

à is also used before someone's name.

> J'ai donné un cadeau *à* Jodie.
> *I gave a present to Jodie.*
>
> ---
>
> Ma mère a envoyé une lettre à sa sœur à Cork.
> *My mother sent a letter to her sister in Cork.*

Just one thing to remember: Although Cork and Limerick are county names, they are also towns, which is why we use **à**. If, on the other hand, you simply wanted to say *I live in the county of* Cork or Limerick, or indeed any other county in Ireland, you would say **J'habite dans le comté de** Cork/Limerick/Wexford, etc.

4.4 What if you need to say *to the* or *at the*?

So you need *to the* or *at the*. What do you do?

> Example: We went *to the* cinema or my aunt is *at the* station.

Well, we have a solution. You use either **au**, **à la**, **à l'** or **aux**. As usual, you need to take into account if the noun following these words is masculine or feminine, singular or plural. Check out the changes:

à+le	⋯⋯>	au	⋯⋯>	Nous allons **au** cinéma. *We are going to the cinema.*
à+la	⋯⋯>	à la	⋯⋯>	Nous attendons le train **à la** gare. *We are waiting for the train at the station.*
à+l'	⋯⋯>	à +l'	⋯⋯>	Mon frère est **à** l'hôpital. *My brother is in hospital.*
à+les	⋯⋯>	aux	⋯⋯>	Je vais **aux** magasins. *I am going to the shops.*

Exercise 4

Write in the correct form of **à** in the following sentences. Try to reason out if you are saying *to the* or *at the* or is it simply *to* or *at*:

> *Example:*   Nous allons _____ marché.
>
> Think! We are not going *to market*, we are going *to the market*.
>
> Nous allons **au** marché.

1. Nous allons souvent _____ Wexford.
2. Mon petit frère va _____ école avec ses amis.
3. Ma tante et mes cousins arriveront _____ gare.
4. Est-ce que tu peux acheter du chocolat _____ supermarché ?
5. Mes tantes et ma mère aiment aller _____ café en ville.
6. Shane doit aller _____ hôpital.
7. Les touristes vont _____ office du tourisme.
8. J'ai envoyé un message _____ Katie.
9. La pâtisserie se trouve _____ Dingle.
10. Nous voulons acheter des croissants _____ la boulangerie.

4.5 Introducing chez

When you want to say that you are going to a particular place, you can use either:

1. **à** + the name of the place, like we saw above.

> Je vais à la boulangerie.   *I am going to the baker's.*
> Elle va à la boucherie.   *She is going to the butcher's.*

OR

2. the preposition **chez**, which means to the shop of:

> Je vais chez le boulanger.   *I am going to the baker's.*
> Elle va chez le boucher.   *I am going to the butcher's.*

In 2 above, the name of the person is used rather than the place.

Maybe you have used **chez** already?

> Je vais chez Marc.   *I am going to Mark's house* or *Mark's place.*

We often use it to say I am going to someone's house, or someone's place without actually mentioning the word **maison**. In Ireland, people sometimes give their house the name **chez moi** *(my place)* or **chez nous** *(our place).*

4.6 De, meaning of or from

De is another tiny, but really useful, preposition. It is used:

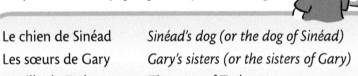

> In English, we use the apostrophe or the word *of* to get across the idea of possession.

1 Before the name of a person/place.

2 When you need to say *of* or *from* a person/thing:

> | Le chien de Sinéad | *Sinéad's dog (or the dog of Sinéad)* |
> | Les sœurs de Gary | *Gary's sisters (or the sisters of Gary)* |
> | La ville de Tralee | *The town of Tralee* |

4.7 What if you need to say of the or from the?

Obviously, we won't always have a proper noun (name of a person or place, e.g. John, Laura, Galway, Cork). What would you use to say the pets *of the* children, the boy's dog? You use either **du, de la, de l'** and **des**. Again you need to take into account whether the noun following these words is masculine or feminine, singular or plural. Check out what happens:

De +le ···⫶	du	···⫶	Le chien du garçon. *The boy's dog (the dog of the boy).*
De +la ···⫶	de la	···⫶	La trousse de la fille. *The girl's pencil case (the pencil case of the girl).*
De +l' ···⫶	de l'	···⫶	Le chat de l'homme. *The man's cat (the cat of the man).*
De+ les ···⫶	des	···⫶	Les manteaux des enfants. *The children's coats (the coats of the children).*

4.8 De + the possessive adjective

When we use **de** with **mon**, **ma**, **mes**, **ton**, **ta**, **tes**, etc. we don't make any changes.

> Le chien de mon frère. *My brother's dog (the dog of my brother).*
>
> La voiture de mon père. *My dad's car (the car of my dad).*

Exercise 5

Write the correct form of **de** in the following sentences. Remember the rules above.

> *Example:* Alex est l'ami _____ Sarah.
>
> Think for a second. You are not going to say Alex is the friend of *the* Sarah! So the correct answer is simply **de**, meaning *of.*
>
> Alex est l'ami **de** Sarah

1 C'est le lapin _____ Barry.

2 Est-ce que vous avez visité le château _____ Dublin ?

3 Les pages _____ livres sont sales !

4 Ma sœur Eleanor est la cadette _____ famille.

5 Le chat _____ enfant est mignon.

6 Mon oncle John est le frère _____ ma mère.

7 Le correspondant _____ ma sœur reste chez nous.

8 John est l'ami _____ Nicole.

9 Les vaches _____ fermiers sont aux champs.

10 Le chien _____ homme est agressif.

A vos marques, prêt, partez !
On your marks, get set ... go!

Exercise 6
Sprint test:

Revise **de**, **à** and all the other prepositions above for twenty minutes.
Hand this book over to a family member/friend to test you ... go on!
Now try to complete this sprint test in 10 minutes.

Write the French word for the following prepositions:

on _____

under _____

in front of _____

behind _____

opposite _____

at the end of _____

near _____

on the outskirts _____

between _____

beside _____

Exercise 7

Forms of **à** when we say *to the* or *at the*

Masculine singular noun	Feminine singular noun	Masculine/feminine before a noun starting with a vowel or silent h	All plural nouns
au	_____	_____	_____

Exercise 8

Forms of **de** when we say *of the* or *from the* are:

Masculine singular noun	Feminine singular noun	Masculine/feminine before a noun starting with a vowel or silent h	All plural nouns
du	_____	_____	_____

4.9 Les prépositions franglais

The word **franglais** is made from the words **Français** and **Anglais**. It refers to French and English words used together.

Exercise 9

The following crossword has clues in both French and English. First, work out the correct *French preposition* and then place it correctly in the puzzle.

Across

4 Mon cartable est (under) _____ ma table.

5 Je suis (in front of) _____ la porte.

6 Je vais (to the) _____ le boucher.

Down

1 Mon école est (at the end of) _____ la rue.

2 Il vient (from) _____ États-Unis.

3 Mon grand-père habite (with) _____ nous.

4.10 A quick word before we finish

Other expressions using **de** and **à**.

There are expressions and phrases in French that cannot be translated word-for-word. The correct term for them is *idiomatic phrases*. Take a look at the examples:

You have probably learned the expression **j'ai quatorze ans** – *I am 14.* This actually translates as *I have fourteen years*, but of course we say *I am 14*.

Je vais bien *I feel fine.* You have probably come across this. Literally this translates as *I am going fine* (**aller, je vais**) but of course it makes more sense in English to say *I feel fine*.

> Be sure to revise the points here on **jouer de**, **jouer à** and **faire de**. You will use these quite a bit!

Idiomatic expressions using *à*

Avoir mal à	*to have a sore (part of your body)*
Il a mal à la tête/au dos/aux dents.	*He has a headache/backache/toothache.*

à+le =au
à+la = à+la
à+les =aux

Rappel !

Jouer à	*to play team sports*
Je joue au rugby/nous jouons au tennis.	*I play rugby/we play tennis.*

Idiomatic expressions using *de*

| | de+le =du |
| de+la =de la |
| de+les =des |
| de+l'= de l' |

Rappel !

| Avoir besoin de | *to need* |
| Nous avons besoin de boire quelque chose. | *We need a drink.* |

| Avoir de la chance | *to have luck* |
| J'ai gagné le prix, j'ai de la chance. | *(we would say to be lucky).* |

Avoir peur de	*to have fear*
	(we would say to be afraid).
J'ai peur des chiens.	*I'm afraid of dogs.*

Jouer de	*to play instruments*
Je joue de la guitare.	*I play the guitar.*
Mon frère joue du violon.	*My brother plays the violin.*

Faire de	for sports that are not played as a team.
Ils font du cyclisme.	The translation is *they cycle*, not *they do cycling*.
Nous faisons du golf.	The translation is we *play golf*, not *we do golf*.

Exercise 10

Can you translate the following sentences into French?
Identify the correct idiomatic expression you need first of all:

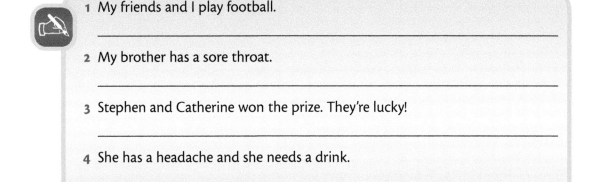

1 My friends and I play football.

_____

2 My brother has a sore throat.

_____

3 Stephen and Catherine won the prize. They're lucky!

_____

4 She has a headache and she needs a drink.

_____

5 We will play golf on holidays.

_____

And a pat on the back!
Well done, let's do a check.

Récapitulez

Check	✓
I am familiar with the keywords at the beginning of the chapter	☐
I understand the three groups of prepositions that indicate location of an object, a place or another relationship	☐
I understand the workings of the preposition **à**	☐
Also the preposition **de**	☐
I have recognised there are phrases using **à** or **de** that do not translate directly. I know these are called idiomatic phrases	☐

Chapter 5
Les Conjonctions
Conjunctions

Key words

···⟩ Linking words   ···⟩ Co-ordinating conjunctions

···⟩ Dependant clauses   ···⟩ Subordinating conjunctions

5.1   A quick word

Answer truthfully! Does your mind boggle when words like conjunctions and prepositions are mentioned? Like most students, it probably does. These grammar terms frequently get mixed up. However, chances are you have been using them all along without even knowing it. Do the words *and*, *but* and *or* ring a bell? Can you remember the definition?

In this chapter, we will focus on the conjunctions you will use a lot. Let's start with the definition:

> **Conjunctions are linking words between two words or phrases.**

Like, for example, the words:

> **mais** *but*   **et** *and*   **parce que** *because*

Chances are, you will find you know many of the words already! In this chapter, we will take a look at the conjunctions you will come across most often in French.

5.2 The most commonly used conjunctions

The most common French conjunctions are:

ainsi que	*as well as*	* ni ... ni ... ne	*neither, nor*
après que	*after*	ou	*or*
comme	*as*	pendant que	*while*
dès que	*as soon as*	puis	*then*
donc	*therefore*	parce que/car	*because*
et	*and*	quand	*when*
mais	*but*	si	*if*

Do not confuse the spelling of **ou** (*or*) with **où** (*where*)

* Did you notice the conjunction **ni** plus **ni** and **ne?**
Strange looking, isn't it? It means *neither/nor*.
We will be talking about it more in the chapter
on negation.

Take a look at some simple sentences
showing their linking function.

You should be saying to yourself,
yes, I can do that, and *that one* and
yes, that one too!

5.3 Functions of conjunctions

Take a look at the following sentences to see conjunctions in action.

Yes, it does rhyme!

> J'aime les framboises *et* les fraises.
> *I like raspberries and strawberries.*
>
> ---
>
> Il *ne* mange *ni* les frites *ni* les pommes de terre.
> *He eats neither chips nor potatoes.*
>
> ---
>
> Est-ce que tu voudrais du café *ou* du thé ?
> *Would you like coffee or tea?*
>
> ---
>
> Damian *et* Jessie regardent la télé.
> *Damian and Jessie are watching television.*
>
> ---
>
> Je voudrais acheter des vêtements *mais* je n'ai pas d'argent.
> *I would like to buy clothes but I have no money*
>
> ---
>
> Est-ce que tu veux un sandwich *ou* un hamburger ?
> *Do you want a sandwich or a burger?*
>
> ---
>
> Fais tes devoirs, *puis* tu peux aller au cinéma.
> *Do your homework, then you can go to the cinema.*

We say they are *coordinating conjunctions* because of their *linking* function in the sentence.

Conjunctions can also link a phrase to the main sentence, giving us more information.

> J'ai peur **quand** je voyage en avion.
>
> ---
>
> *I am afraid* **when** *I travel by plane.*

The main clause is *I am afraid*. When am I afraid? Not all the time, just when I travel by plane. … **quand je voyage en avion** adds more information to why I am afraid. We say it is the *dependant clause* because it does not make sense by itself. **J'ai peur** gives the sentence its full meaning so that it makes sense.

> Elle dit qu'elle aime le chocolat.
>
> *She said she likes chocolate.*

Here the phrase **qu'elle aime le chocolat** (*that she likes chocolate*) is the dependant clause because it does not make sense by itself. Adding **Elle dit** makes it a proper sentence.

We call **que** and **quand** *subordinating conjunctions* because of the way they join *dependant* or *subordinate* clauses to the main clause.

Si is also used in this way but if you would like to see a fuller explanation of its uses, be sure to refer to the chapters on the future and conditional tenses.

In the chapter on the future tense, we discuss the use of **si**+*present*+*future*.

In the chapter on the conditional tense, we discuss the use of **si** + *imperfect* +*conditional*.

5.4 Future tense after quand and dès que

When **quand** or **dès que** refer to the future, we use the future tense in French whereas we use the present tense in English.

> Je te téléphonerai dès que *j'arriverai* à l'hôtel.
>
> *I'll phone you as soon as I arrive (will arrive) at the hotel.*
>
> ⋯⋮⟩   In French we use the future tense.
>
> Quand je *finirai* mes examens, j'irai en vacances.
>
> *When I finish (will finish) my exams, I will go on holidays.*
>
> ⋯⋮⟩   Future tense of aller

Revision exercises

Exercise 1

1 Choose five conjunctions that you are confident in using from the list on page 84. Write suitable sentences showing their uses.

2 **Les messages :**

Send a text message to your friend Karen in French.

> **Boîte de vocabulaire :**
>
> | | |
> |---|---|
> | Je reste… | *I am staying…* |
> | Je n'ai pas d'argent. | *I have no money.* |
> | Est-ce que tu voudrais ? | *Would you like to?* |
> | Ce soir… | *This evening…* |

- Say you are staying at home because you have no money.

  You then send another message to your friend John.

  You know he has no money either!

- Ask him would he like to watch either the television or a film in your house this evening?

3 A vos marques, prêt, partez ! *On your marks, get set … go!*

Sprint test:

Revise over all the conjunctions above.

You should complete this sprint test in 2–3 minutes.

Write the French word for the following conjunctions:

> but _____
>
> therefore _____
>
> or _____
>
> while _____
>
> if _____
>
> when _____
>
> because _____   or we could use _____
>
> as well as _____
>
> as _____

4 Fill in the gaps with a suitable conjunction from the list. Choose wisely!

Parce que	donc	comme	et	mais
si /s'	comme	ni ... ni ...	quand	dès que

1 Jack ____ Ann iront au supermarché.

2 J'aime aller au restaurant _____ je n'ai pas d'argent.

3 Je te téléphonerai _____ j'aurai des nouvelles.

4 _____ il fait beau, nous irons au match.

5 _____ Susan n'a pas de voiture, elle doit marcher.

6 Tu n'as pas fait tes devoirs, _____ tu ne pourras pas sortir.

7 Nous avons faim _____ nous n'avons pas le temps de manger.

8 J'aide ma mère avec le ménage _____ ma sœur fait ses devoirs.

9 _____ mon ami Jack aura fini son travail, il viendra me voir.

10 _____ mon père _____ ma mère ne peut aller à la réunion.

Now that wasn't too bad, was it? Let's go back quickly over the work done.

Récapitulez

Check	✓
I am familiar with the keywords at the beginning of the chapter	☐
I have learned the definition of a conjunction	☐
I can give at least five examples of conjunctions	☐
I also know how to use them	☐
I know what subordinate or dependant clauses are	☐
I know how to use **quand** and **dès que** with the future tense	☐

Chapter 6
Le Passé Composé
Past (Composed) Tense

Key words

- Perfect tense
- Participe passé
- Imperfect tense
- Helping/Auxilary verb

6.1 A quick word before we begin

You can think of the **passé composé** as being made up of several smaller parts that combine to create the tense.

You may have noticed the title of this chapter. The **passé composé** is one of the past tenses in French. It is also known as the perfect tense. If you want to talk about something you did yesterday, last weekend, last month or any time in the past, you use the **passé composé**.

6.2 Formation of the passé composé

Look back up to the title. It is a composed tense, meaning that there is more than one part to it.

> **This is the reason behind the name.**

Le passé composé is composed of either the auxiliary/helper verb of **avoir** or **être** and the past participle, or **participe passé**, of the verb concerned.

Present tense of **avoir** + *past participle* of the verb = **passé composé**.

J'ai donné.　　　*I gave* or *I have given.*

ai from the present tense of **avoir** and **donné** which is the past participle of the verb **donner**, *to give*.

J'ai fait.　　　*I have done* or *I did.*

Je suis allé(e).　　　*I went* or *I've been.*

This time we are using: Present tense of **être** + *past participle* = **passé composé**.

We are going to divide the chapter into the following parts:

So, according to what you are doing in class and what you want to revise, use this chapter section by section!

Le passé composé 1:	Verbs that take **avoir**
Le passé composé 2:	Irregular verbs that take **avoir** in the **passé composé**
Le passé composé 3:	Verbs that take **être**
Le passé composé 4:	Reflexive verbs in the **passé composé**
Le passé composé 5:	Negatives in the **passé composé**

6.3 Le passé composé 1: Verbs that take avoir

The **passé composé** is formed by using the present tense of **avoir**.

Rappel !

Avoir in the present tense:

j'ai	nous avons
tu as	vous avez
il a	ils ont
elle a	elles ont

Formation of the passé composé with avoir

The past participle is formed as follows.

> If it is an **-er** verb, drop the ending **-er** and add **-é**.
> *Example:*   visiter   ····▸   visité

> If it is an **-ir** verb, drop the ending **-ir** and add **-i**.
> *Example:*   finir   ····▸   fini

> If it is an **-re** verb, drop the ending and add **-u**.
> *Example:*   perdre   ····▸   perdu

Exercise 1

Now, let's practise! Can you identify the correct past participle?

1 Past participle of **finir**	a) finé	b) fini	☐
2 Past participle of **descendre**	a) descendant	b) descendu	☐
3 Past participle of **attendre**	a) attendu	b) attendit	☐
4 Past participle of **manger**	a) mangeant	b) mangé	☐
5 Past participle of **parler**	a) parlé	b) parli	☐
6 Past participle of **vendre**	a) vendu	b) vent	☐

7 Past participle of **regarder**	a) regardu	b) regardé	◯
8 Past participle of **choisir**	a) choisi	b) choisant	◯
9 Past participle of **trouver**	a) trouvé	b) trouvu	◯
10 Past participle of **perdre**	a) perdu	b) pert	◯

Visiter (to visit)

J'ai visité	*I visited/have visited*
Tu as visité	*You visited/have visited*
Il a visité	*He visited/has visited*
Elle a visité	*She visited/has visited*
Nous avons visité	*We visited*
Vous avez visité	*You* (polite/plural) *visited/have visited*
Ils ont visité	*They visited/have visited*
Elles ont visité	*They visited/have visited*

Finir (to finish)

J'ai fini	*I finished/have finished*
Tu as fini	*You finished/have finished*
Il a fini	*He finished/has finished*
Elle a fini	*She finished/has finished*
Nous avons fini	*We finished/have finished*
Vous avez fini	*You finished* (polite plural)
Ils ont fini	*They finished/have finished*
Elles ont fini	*They finished/have finished*

Perdre (to lose)

J'ai perdu	*I lost/have lost*
Tu as perdu	*You lost/have lost*
Il a perdu	*He lost/has lost*
Elle a perdu	*She lost/has lost*
Nous avons perdu	*We lost/have lost*
Vous avez perdu	*You lost/have lost*
Ils ont perdu	*They lost/have lost*
Elles ont perdu	*They lost/have lost*

Exercise 2

Write in the correct form of the verb in the **passé composé** below.

> *Example:*   Il (perdre) son portefeuille.
>
>   Il a perdu son portefeuille.

Note:

N'oublie pas !
There are two parts:
present tense of avoir +
participe passé.

1 Hier, j'_____ _____ (jouer) au basket avec mon équipe.

2 Je _____ _____ (choisir) les choses à manger pour le pique-nique.

3 Tu _____ _____ (vendre) ta voiture ?

4 Vendredi dernier, nous _____ _____ (manger) dans un bon restaurant du quartier.

5 Elles _____ _____ (garder) de bons souvenirs de leurs vacances.

6 Ils _____ _____ (louer) des vélos.

7 Mes amis et moi _____ _____ (bavarder) avant les cours.

8 Les cours _____ _____ (commencer) à 8h 45.

9 Les cours _____ _____ (finir) à 3h 40.

10 Ils _____ _____ (rendre) les livres à la bibliothèque.

6.4 Le passé composé 2: Irregular past participles of verbs that take avoir

Some verbs that take **avoir** in the **passé composé** have irregular past participles and must be learned by heart. (In other words, **-er** verbs do not become **é**, **-ir** verbs do not become **i** and **-re** verbs do not become **u**).

> *Example:*   Faire ⋯⋗ J'ai fait.   *I did.*
>
> Lire ⋯⋗ Mon frère a lu le journal. *My brother read the paper.*

Verbs with irregular past participles

Infinitif	Participe Passé	Passé Composé
Avoir	eu	J'ai eu un accident/*I had an accident.*
Boire	bu	Tu as bu une tasse de thé ?/*Did you drink a cup of tea?*
Devoir	dû	Il a dû aller/*He had to go.*
Écrire	écrit	Elle a écrit une lettre/*She wrote a letter.*
Être	été	Nous avons été malade/*We were sick.*
Faire	fait	Vous avez fait vos devoirs ?/*Did you do your homework?*
Lire	lu	Ils ont lu le journal/*They read the paper.*
Offrir	offert	Elles ont offert des cadeaux/*They offered/gave presents.*
Pouvoir	pu	J'ai pu sortir/*I was able to go.*
Prendre	pris	Tu as pris des photos ?/*Did you take photographs?*
Recevoir	reçu	Il a reçu une lettre/*He received a letter.*
Savoir	su	Elle a su la réponse/*She knew the answer.*
Voir	vu	Nous avons vu le film/*We saw the film.*
Vouloir	voulu	Vous avez voulu sortir ?/*Did you want to go out?*

You will have noticed the **passé composé** of **avoir** and **être** from the table. Although we have been using these as helper verbs, they also have a **passé composé** of their own.

Exercise 3

Choose the correct part of the verb in the following exercise.

Example: Alex (prendre) l'avion à Beauvais.
Alex a pris l'avion à Beauvais.

Note:
N'oublie pas ! No agreement here with the extra 'e' and 's'. That's only for être verbs.

1 Elle _____ _____ (lire) le dernier roman de J.K Rowling.
2 En vacances, j'_____ _____ (écrire) une lettre à mes parents.
3 Chez nous hier soir, ma mère _____ _____ (boire) cinq tasses de café !
4 Simon _____ _____ (devoir) aller au travail.
5 Nous _____ _____ (rire) plusieurs fois pendant le spectacle.
6 Ma sœur _____ _____ (voir) le film hier soir.
7 Mes parents _____ _____ (dire) que je pouvais aller en vacances avec mes amis !
8 Claudine _____ _____ (vouloir) acheter un Nintendo DS.
9 Il _____ _____ (prendre) des photos.
10 Tous les élèves _____ _____ (savoir) la réponse.

6.5 Le passé composé 3: Verbs that take être

How do you know which verbs form the **passé composé** with **être**?

The following are the sixteen verbs that use **être** instead of **avoir** to form the **passé composé**. They are **mainly** concerned with movement.

> **Être** in the present tense
>
> | | |
> |---|---|
> | je suis | nous sommes |
> | tu es | vous êtes |
> | il est | ils sont |
> | elle est | elles sont |

Try to remember the first letter of each verb in this way:

MR VANS TRRRAMPPED

Monter (*to go up*)	**Venir** (*to come*)	**Tomber** (*to fall*)
Rentrer (*to return*)	**Aller** (*to go*)	**Retourner** (*to return*)
	Naître (*to be born*)	**Revenir** (*to come back*)
	Sortir (*to go out*)	**Rester** (*to stay*)
		Arriver (*to arrive*)
		Mourir (*to die*)
		Partir (*to leave*)
		*Passer (*to come by*)
		Entrer (*to enter*)
		Descendre (*to go down*)

Learn these **par cœur** !

Calmez-Vous !

We still drop the **-er**, **-ir** and **-re** so nothing changes there.

It is still made up of a helping or auxiliary verb, this time it is **être** instead of **avoir**.

So far so good! Now for the changes.

Now, take a look at the table of MR VANS TRRRAMPPED with the corresponding participe passé.

Verbe	Participe Passé	Verbe	Participe Passé
Aller (*to go*)	allé	Venir (*to come*)	venu
Arriver (*to arrive*)	arrivé	Partir (*to leave*)	parti
Entrer (*to go in*)	entré	Sortir (*to go out*)	sorti
*Monter (*to go up*)	monté	*Descendre (*to go down*)	descendu
Naître (*to be born*)	né	Mourir (*to die*)	mort
Tomber (*to fall*)	tombé	*Passer (*to drop by*)	passé
Rentrer (*to go home*)	rentré	Rester (*to stay*)	resté
Revenir (*to come back*)	revenu	Retourner (*to return*)	retourné

* **Passer** has three meanings: to drop by/to sit exams/to spend time.

1 When **passer** means to drop by, it takes **être**.

Je *suis* passé chez toi.   *I dropped by your house.*

2 When **passer** means to sit exams, it takes **avoir**.

J'*ai* passé mes examens hier.   *I sat my exams yesterday.*

*When **passer** means to spend time, it also takes **avoir**.*

J'*ai* passé trois semaines en France.   *I spent three weeks in France.*

3 **Monter** and **descendre** can take **avoir** at times.

Elle est montée.   *She went up.*

Elle a monté les valises.   *She took the suitcases upstairs.*

Elle est descendue.   *She came down.*

Elle a descendu les valises.   *She brought the suitcases down.*

Remember, when **avoir** is used there is no agreement.

Tips

Devenir *to become*, and **Revenir** *to come back*, are also done like this. It is simply the verb **venir** with **de** and **re** before it. It is conjugated exactly like **venir** but with an extra attachment at the beginning!

e.g.	Je suis venu.	*I came.*
	Je suis devenu.	*I became.*
	Je suis revenu.	*I came back.*

And one other thing.

No, you didn't imagine those little brackets with the extra **e** in them!

*With **être** verbs in the* **passé composé**, *there is always agreement between the subject and the past participle.*

You add:

- **nothing** when the subject is masculine singular (il).
- an extra **e** when the subject is feminine singular (elle).
- an extra **s** when the subject is masculine plural (ils);
  this can also be used for a group of boys and girls.

- An extra **es** when the subject is feminine plural (elles) or
  when using **vous** to refer to a group of females.

So again, this is a really important idea to understand. If a verb takes **être** as its helper verb in the **passé composé**, we must add:

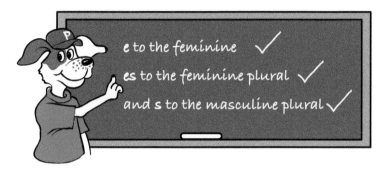

Take a look at the verb **aller** fully worked out:

Aller in the **passé composé**	
Je suis allé(e)	*I went/I have gone* (extra **e** if it is a female speaking).
Tu es allé(e)	*You went/have gone* (extra **e** again if you are speaking about a female).
Il est allé	*He went/has gone* (nothing out of the ordinary here!).
Elle est allée	*She went/has gone* (always an extra **e**, as it is about a girl).
Nous sommes allé(e)s	*We went/have gone* (an extra **e** if talking about a group of girls, **always** an s).
Vous êtes allé(e)(s)	*You went/have gone* 1 an extra **e** if we are talking about a girl in the polite form 2 an extra **s** if we are talking about the plural form 3 and third option would be both the extra **e** and the **s** if we are talking about a group of females
Ils sont allés	*They went/have gone* (group of boys/men).
Elles sont allées	*They went/have gone* (group of girls).

Exercise 4

Now can you fill in the following table?

	Aller	Sortir	Venir	Monter	Descendre	Tomber	Rester
Je							
Tu							
Il							
Elle							
Nous							
Vous							
Ils							
Elles							
Marc et Sophie							
Anna et Suzie							
Luc et Paul							

Another quick word

A question students often ask when doing practice exercises on the **passé composé** is how do I know if the pronoun **je** or **nous** is masculine or feminine? Unless indicated otherwise, presume it is masculine.

Exercise 5

Fill in the correct part of the verb.

> *Example:*   J' ___ ___ (arriver) hier.
>
>   Je suis arrivé hier.   *I arrived yesterday.*

Note:

N'oublie pas !
There are two parts,
present tense of **être**
+ **participe passé**.

1 Mon ami Peter _____ _____ (naître) en Angleterre.

2 Elle _____ _____ (aller) au match.

3 Elles _____ _____ (arriver) en retard.

4 Hier soir, je _____ _____ (sortir) avec mes amis.

5 Tu _____ _____ (partir) ?

6 Gina _____ _____ (retourner) vers 20h à la maison.

7 Nous _____ _____ (aller) en ville avec la bande.

8 Mon grand-père _____ _____ (mourir) quand j'avais dix ans.

9 Vous _____ _____ (monter) dans le train à Athlone ?

10 Ils _____ _____ (partir) de bonne heure.

6.6 **Le passé composé 4: Reflexive verbs**

All reflexive verbs are conjugated with **être** in the past tense. So again, the rule applies where the verbs must agree with the subject of the verb in gender and in number.

> *Example:*   Je me suis lev**é** à 7 heures ce matin.   *(I, boy/man speaking)*
>
>   Je me suis lev**ée** à 7 heures ce matin.   *(I, girl/woman speaking)*

Let's pause for a minute and reflect!

As we seem to be talking a lot about subjects and objects, let's clarify a few things:

- The *personal pronoun* or *noun* (*je, tu, il, Ciara, Mark et Niamh*, etc.) is the *subject* of the verb.
- Looking back to the example above, who got up? Well, I did, so that makes me the subject, the person who did the action of getting up.
- The *me* is the *direct object pronoun*, meaning myself. Who did I get up? Myself, of course, so that makes myself the *object* of the sentence.

Rappel !

> The reflexive pronouns are **me/te/se/nous/vous/se.**

> *Example:*   Il s'est levé.   *He got himself up.*

Remember the columns we talked about in the chapter on the present tense? Well, let's use the idea again here. It is really useful to help visualise how many parts we need for reflexive verbs in the present tense.

Let's take a look at the verb **se lever** in this way.

1	2	3	4
Je	me	suis	levé (e)
Tu	t'	es	levé (e)
Il	s'	est	levé
Elle	s'	est	levée
Nous	nous	sommes	levé(e)s
Vous	vous	êtes	levé(e) (s)
Ils	se	sont	levés
Elles	se	sont	levées

Now try to 'take in' a worked example of this verb as it usually appears.

Se lever – *to get oneself up*	
Je me suis levé (e)	Nous nous sommes levé(e)s
Tu t'es levé (e)	Vous vous êtes levé(e)(s)
Il s'est levé	Ils se sont levés
Elle s'est levée	Elles se sont levées

Remember you must have four parts to these verbs in the **passé composé**!

Other reflexive verbs are

S'amuser	*to have a good time*
Se brosser	*to brush one's teeth*
Se dépêcher	*to hurry*
Se disputer	*to argue*
S'habiller	*to get dressed*
S'imaginer	*to imagine*
Se laver	*to wash*
Se moquer	*to mock*
Se préparer	*to prepare*

Exercise 6

Write the correct form of the verb in brackets in the **passé composé**, don't forget to change the pronoun!

Note:
N'oublie pas !
Remember, there are four parts, 3 to fill in!

Example: Nous _____ _____ _____ (s'amuser) en vacances.
Nous nous sommes amusés en vacances.

1 Je _____ _____ _____ (se coucher) à minuit.
2 Vous _____ _____ _____ (s'amuser) au concert ?
3 Ils _____ _____ _____ (se lever) très tôt ce matin.
4 Je _____ _____ _____ (se laver). (*Je = female*)
5 Kate et Amy _____ _____ _____ (se promener).
6 Elles _____ _____ _____ (s'habiller).
7 Tu _____ _____ _____ (se coucher) tard.
8 Dean _____ _____ _____ (se lever) de bonne heure.
9 Nous _____ _____ _____ (se balader) à la campagne.

6.7 Le passé composé 5: Negatives in the passé composé

The rule to learn

Ne comes before the first part of the verb, and the negative word
(let's take **pas** as the example here) comes after it.

> Ne + Pas = *Not*

In the **passé composé** the first part of the verb is of course the helping verb.

> *Example:*   Je ne suis pas allé au match.   *I did not go to the match.*
>
>   Je ne suis jamais allé en Italie.   *I have never been to Italy.*

There are other negative forms such as **ne** and **plus**, *no more* and **ne** and
que, *only*, but we will deal with those in chapter 12. For the purpose of the
exercises here you will need to know:

> **ne + pas** = *not*
> **ne + jamais** = *never*

Exercise 7

Using **ne** and **pas**, write the following sentences in the negative:

> *Example:*   Nous avons fait le ménage.
>
>   Nous n'avons pas fait le ménage.

1 J'ai lu le roman. _____

2 Nous avons joué au foot. _____

3 Je suis allé en ville. _____

4 Il a travaillé à Aer Lingus. _____

5 Elle a acheté des CD. _____

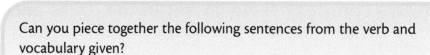

Can you piece together the following sentences from the verb and vocabulary given?

You will need to use either **ne** + **pas** or **ne** + **jamais**.

6 The train did not leave on time.   (partir … à l'heure)

7 We did not arrive by taxi.   (arriver … en taxi)

8 She never comes out with us.   (sortir … avec nous)

9 He never got up early during the holidays.   (se lever … tôt … pendant les vacances)

10 They did not play football yesterday.   (jouer … au foot … hier)

6.8   Order is important

Ok! Now you are probably thinking there are a lot of parts to a negative structure in the **passé composé**. Yet, we have a solution to make remembering them a little easier.

We're going to learn a little rhyme here. This little tune is going to grow in size as we add in some pronouns in a later chapter. Here, however, we just need to remember a little part of it. It goes like this:

> **Je**   *before* **ne**   *before* **me**   *before* **verb**   *before* **pas**

A clarification:

Here we are just saying **Je**, but the **Je** is representative of all the other personal pronouns. Take a look at it in its extended form:

Je	ne	me	suis	pas
Tu		te (t')	es	
Il		se (s')		
Elle		se (s')		
Nous		nous		
Vous		vous		
Ils		se (s')		
Elles		se (s')		

Then we have the **participe passé** of the verb, e.g. fait, allé.

Chantons !

Try singing it!

Revision exercises

This phrase was at the beginning of the chapter:

'You can think of the **passé composé** as being made up of several smaller parts that combine to create the tense.'

composed tense

avoir

être

Having studied all the smaller parts, we now need to piece them together.

The aim of the following exercises is to make sure you understand the logic of the passé composé.

When you have answered the questions below, try to explain the answers to a friend. If you can explain it well, then you understand it. So over to you!

1 Explain the title **Le passé composé** in your own words.

2 Write out the verb **arriver** in the **passé composé**. Explain each agreement as you conjugate it.

3 Using **s'amuser**, give a one-sentence example to illustrate:

   the subject of the verb
   the object of the verb
   the auxiliary verb
   the **participe passé**

4 What does the little tune **je** *before* **ne** *before* **me** *before* verb *before* **pas** aim to explain? Show what each part is representative of.

In the following exercise, choose the form of the verb that you think is correct. Revise which verbs take être in the past tense!

1 Tu **as/es** arrivé très tard. _____

2 Nous **avons/sommes** voyagé en France ensemble. _____

3 Il **s'est/a** brossé les dents. _____

4 Peter **est/a** déménagé à Galway. _____

5 Le petit bébé **est/a** né hier. _____

6 Les garçons **ont/sont** joué pendant la récréation. _____

7 Nous **sommes/avons** restés en ville pendant toute la journée. _____

8 Nous **avons/sommes** marché jusqu'à l'école. _____

9 Il **a/est** raté son examen. _____

10 Fiona **est/a** tombée pendant
le cours d'aérobique. _____

Give the passé composé of the verb in brackets.

11 Les jumeaux de ma tante _____ _____ (naître) en juillet.

12 Mon ami, Jack, _____ _____ (partir) faire le tour du monde.

13 Elle _____ _____ (chercher) les clés partout.

14 Mon frère et moi _____ _____ (prendre) le car à 8h.

15 Il _____ _____ (pleuvoir) cet après-midi.

Now can you say what the correct past participle of the following verbs are?

16 **Courir** a) couru b) couri ☐

17 **Dire** a) dit b) du ☐

18 **Devoir** a) du b) dû ☐

19 **Connaître** a) connu b) connaîtu ☐

20 **Prendre** a) pris b) prit ☐

Now you need to think back on this chapter and make sure you can, truthfully put a tick beside the items on the checklist:

Récapitulez

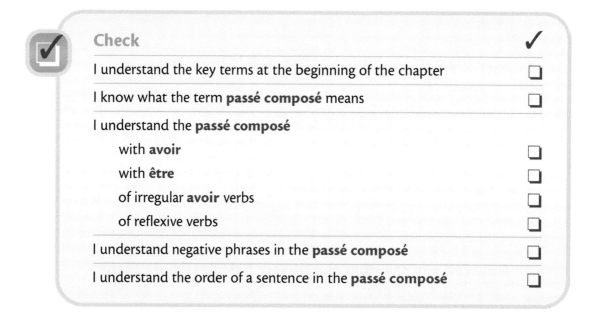

Check	✓
I understand the key terms at the beginning of the chapter	☐
I know what the term **passé composé** means	☐
I understand the **passé composé**	
with **avoir**	☐
with **être**	☐
of irregular **avoir** verbs	☐
of reflexive verbs	☐
I understand negative phrases in the **passé composé**	☐
I understand the order of a sentence in the **passé composé**	☐

Chapter 7
Les Adverbes
Adverbs

Key words

···▷ Verb   ···▷ Manner

···▷ Action   ···▷ Invariable

···▷ Adverb

7.1 A quick word before we begin

How did you get up this morning? What about the Monday morning you actually thought was Saturday! You probably got up *slowly*, *reluctantly* and very *gradually* as you hit your snooze button five times!

> An adverb is what we add on to the verb to tell us more about it. As an adjective describes a noun, an adverb describes a verb.

ad+verb = **adverb**

The action here is the getting up.
The *slowly, reluctantly, gradually* are the adverbs, as they tell you more about the verb. In English these adverbs are usually *ly* words.

7.2 Definition of an adverb

Have you learned this definition? The following is the simplest way to explain adverbs:

> **An adverb is a word that tells us more about a verb.**

Usually, when we talk about adverbs, we mean adverbs of *manner*.

> Why **manner**? It is because they explain the way or the **manner** in which something is done.

Example:	I got up *slowly*.	⋯⟩	How you got up/the *manner* in which you got up.
	I ate my breakfast *quickly*.	⋯⟩	How you ate your breakfast/ the *manner* in which you ate your breakfast.

The main adverbs you must know are listed in the following pages.

In French we usually add on **ment** to the feminine of the adjective (See Group 1 on page 113). Mostly, adverbs are *invariable*, meaning we do not need to worry about changing them to masculine or feminine. Once you've got the adverb and learned it, that's it!

7.3 Formation of adverbs

Adverbs are usually formed from adjectives. We are simply taking the adjective and twisting it around a bit. Its roots are in the original adjective word. From the previous examples, we can see this. *Slowly* has come from the adjective *slow* and *quickly* has come from the adjective *quick*.

A slow get up	⋯⋮⋯▶	I got up slowly
⋮⋮▼		⋮⋮▼
Here *slow* is the adjective, describing the getting up from bed.		*Slowly* is the adverb describing the manner in which you got out of bed.

Let's take a look at how these adverbs of manner are formed in French. There are five groups. These contain the main adverbs you will come across:

Group 1

Add **ment** to the feminine form of the adjective. Usually, we add **ment** to the feminine form of the adjective. It goes like this:

> Pronunciation: pronounce the **ment** like *mong* in English.

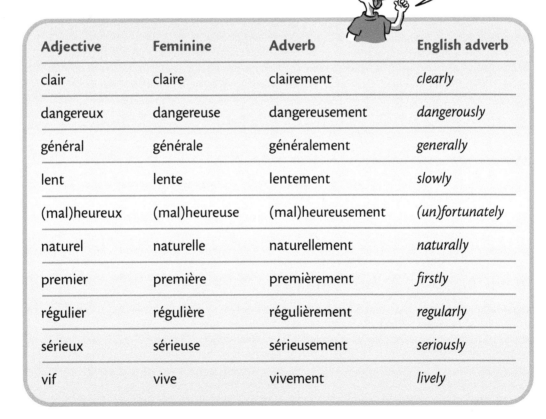

Adjective	Feminine	Adverb	English adverb
clair	claire	clairement	*clearly*
dangereux	dangereuse	dangereusement	*dangerously*
général	générale	généralement	*generally*
lent	lente	lentement	*slowly*
(mal)heureux	(mal)heureuse	(mal)heureusement	*(un)fortunately*
naturel	naturelle	naturellement	*naturally*
premier	première	premièrement	*firstly*
régulier	régulière	régulièrement	*regularly*
sérieux	sérieuse	sérieusement	*seriously*
vif	vive	vivement	*lively*

There are two exceptions to this. They end in **ment** but their stem in the feminine form of the adjective is irregular. Do you see the irregular feminine adjective?

bref	brève	**brièvement**	*briefly*
gentil	gentille	**gentiment**	*gently*

Group 2

Adjectives that end in a vowel.

If the adjective ends in a vowel, we don't need to go through all of this transformation process. Instead we add **ment** to the adjective as it is.

Adjective	Adverb	Adverb in English
absolu	absolument	*absolutely*
confortable	confortablement	*comfortably*
facile	facilement	*easily*
poli	poliment	*politely*
spontané	spontanément	*spontaneously*
vrai	vraiment	*truly*

What do the above have in common? Yes, all of the these adverbs in Group 1 and 2 have a vowel immediately before the **-ment** ending.

Lot of the "mm"s here!

Group 3

Adjectives that end in **ant** or **ent**.

With this group, we remove the **ant** or **ent** from the original adjective and add **amment** or **emment**.

Adjective	Adverb	Adverb in English
apparent	apparemment	*apparently*
bruyant	bruyamment	*noisily*
constant	constamment	*constantly*
intelligent	intelligemment	*intelligently*
patient	patiemment	*patiently*
suffisant	suffisamment	*sufficiently*

Group 4

Slightly irregular adverbs.

The following adverbs are just a bit different. Yes they do have the **-ment** ending and yes they do have the vowel, an **e**, before the **-ment** ending but they take an **acute accent** (**é**) on this **e**:

Adjective	Adverb	Adverb in English
aveugle	aveuglément	*blindly*
commun	communément	*commonly*
confus	confusément	*confusedly*
énorme	énormément	*enormously*
intense	intensément	*intensely*
obscur	obscurément	*obscurely*
précis	précisément	*precisely*
profond	profondément	*profoundly*
uniforme	uniformément	*uniformly*

Group 5

The bandit group.

Now let's look at the downright irregular ones. These are completely lawless and show no concern for rules. They are adjectives of manner but do not end in **ment**:

Adjective	Adverb	Adverb in English
bon	bien	*good* has become *well*
mauvais	mal	*bad* has become *badly*
meilleur	mieux	*better* has become *best*
rapide	*vite	*quick* has become *fast*

*We can also use **rapidement** *(rapidly)* here.

7.4 Position of adverbs

Adverbs usually follow the verb.

> *Example:*   Nous travaillons bien.   *We work well.*

In compound tenses like the **passé composé** or the **futur proche**, we slot the adverb between the auxiliary and the verb.

Rappel !

> A compound tense has two or more parts. The auxiliary verb is the helping verb of **avoir** or **être** for the **passé composé** or **aller** for the **futur proche**.

> Nous avons bien travaillé.   *We worked well.*
>
> Nous allons bien travailler.   *We are going to work well.*

Longer adverbs, like those in Groups 1–4, can be placed at the beginning or the end of the sentence:

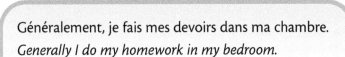

In English, too, it makes more sense to put adjectives like 'generally' and 'unfortunately' at the beginning or end of a sentence.

> Généralement, je fais mes devoirs dans ma chambre.
> *Generally I do my homework in my bedroom.*
>
> ---
>
> Ma sœur est malade, malheureusement.
> *My sister is sick, unfortunately.*

When you have a negative sentence, adverbs, which would normally follow the verb, are placed after **pas**.

> Il mange trop/Il ne mange pas trop.
> *He eats too much/he doesn't eat too much.*
>
> ---
>
> Elle a bien travaillé/Elle n'a pas bien travaillé.
> *She works well/she doesn't work well.*
>
> ---
>
> Ray marche vite/Ray ne marche pas vite.
> *Ray walks fast/Ray doesn't walk fast.*

Revision exercises

Exercise 1

A vos marques, prêt, partez !
On your marks, get set ... go!

The next exercise means you have
to be quick off the mark.

To get maximum value out of this sprint test,
you should make sure you are clear about the rules
for forming adverbs. It's a race. Be quick!

Vas-y vite ! *Quickly!*
Can you spot the
adverb here?

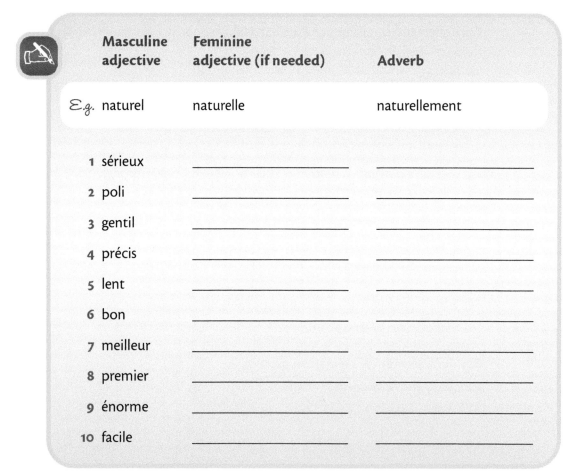

	Masculine adjective	Feminine adjective (if needed)	Adverb
E.g.	naturel	naturelle	naturellement
1	sérieux	_____	_____
2	poli	_____	_____
3	gentil	_____	_____
4	précis	_____	_____
5	lent	_____	_____
6	bon	_____	_____
7	meilleur	_____	_____
8	premier	_____	_____
9	énorme	_____	_____
10	facile	_____	_____

Exercise 2

Change the adjectives below in brackets into an adverb. You then need to place it correctly in the sentence. All verbs are in the present tense.

E.g. John marche au lycée. (lent ⋯⋙ lentement)
John marche lentement au lycée. *John walks slowly to school.*

1 Elle va au supermarché. (régulier ⋯⋙ _____)

_____

2 Je parle aux voisins. (poli ⋯⋙ _____)

_____

3 Le professeur explique les devoirs. (clair ⋯⋙ _____)

_____

4 Michael joue pendant le match. (courageux ⋯⋙ _____)

_____

5 La voiture roule. (rapide ⋯⋙ _____)

_____

6 Ma sœur joue du piano. (constant ⋯⋙ _____)

_____

7 Je travaille pour le professeur
de français. (bon ⋯⋙ _____)

_____

8 Le chat court après la souris. (aveugle ⋯⋙ _____)

_____

9 Je suis malade. (malheureux ⋯⋙ _____)
(Hint: think where the adverb would make the most sense in this sentence.)

_____

10 Les étudiants vont au lycée. (lent ⋯⋙ _____)

_____

And here we are at the end! Now that you have got to this stage, let's take a look back over the work.

Récapitulez

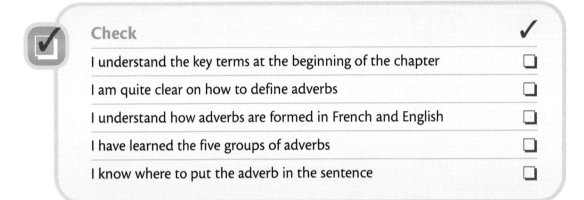

Check	✓
I understand the key terms at the beginning of the chapter	☐
I am quite clear on how to define adverbs	☐
I understand how adverbs are formed in French and English	☐
I have learned the five groups of adverbs	☐
I know where to put the adverb in the sentence	☐

Chapter 8
L'imparfait
The Imperfect Tense

Key words

- ⋯⟫ Perfect actions
- ⋯⟫ Imperfect actions
- ⋯⟫ Description
- ⋯⟫ Background
- ⋯⟫ Story/Narrative
- ⋯⟫ Complement
- ⋯⟫ Context

8.1 A quick word

In this chapter, we talk about a past tense called the **imparfait**, or imperfect tense.

The **passé composé** is used to indicate an action that is clearly over and completed in the past. It is because of this idea of completeness that we call it the perfect tense.

On the other hand, we have **l'imparfait** or the **imperfect** tense. This tense is used for a repeated or an incomplete action, or to describe how someone was at a time in the past. It is because of this uncertainty of a clear beginning and end that we call it the imperfect tense.

In this sense there is nothing perfect about it!

So far, so good! The rules seem pretty simple. Let's look at the relationship between the **passé composé** and the **imparfait**.

Imparfait	**je donnais**, translates as	*I was giving/I used to give.*
Passé Composé	**j'ai donné**, translates as	*I gave, or I have given.*

The action in the **imparfait** is incomplete; we are not sure when the beginning or ending is.

8.2 Formation of verbs in the imparfait

(Refer back to the chapter 3 on the Present Tense here, for reminders of the **nous** *form of verbs.)*

Take the **nous** *form of the verb in the present tense* (even if it is an irregular verb) and remove its ending, then add **ais**, **ais**, **ait**, **ions**, **iez** and **aient**.

> An example of a regular verb in the present:
>
> *Example:* **Donner** ⋯⟩ Nous donn~~ons~~ ⋯⟩ donn ⋯⟩ Je donn**ais** *(to give)*

> An example of an irregular verb in the present:
>
> *Example:* **Faire** ⋯⟩ Nous fais~~ons~~ ⋯⟩ fais ⋯⟩ Je fais**ais** *(to do)*

See? We still go to the **nous** form of the verb even if it is irregular in the present tense.

Exercise 1: Verb sprint

Before you attempt this exercise, you should quickly revise the present tense to give you the best possible chance of 100%!

Example: Regarder ···⟩ **nous** form in present is **nous regardons** ···⟩
Je form in **imparfait** is the stem, **regard** ···⟩ and the **je**
form in the **imparfait** is **regard + ais**, **je regardais**

	Nous form in present tense	**Je** form in the **imparfait**
Parler	nous _____	Je _____
Choisir	nous _____	Je _____
Vendre	nous _____	Je _____
Habiter	nous _____	Je _____
Jouer	nous _____	Je _____
Avoir	nous _____	Je _____
Aller	nous _____	Je _____
Faire	nous _____	Je _____
Finir	nous _____	Je _____
Lire	nous _____	Je _____

Example: **Courir** – *to run*
(**Nous courons**, irregular present tense verb ···⟩ **courons** ···⟩ **cour**)

Je courais	*I used to run/was running*
Tu courais	*You used to run/was running*
Il courait	*He used to run/was running*
Elle courait	*She used to run/was running*
Nous courions	*We used to run/were running*
Vous couriez	*You used to run/were running*
Ils couraient	*They used to run/were running*
Elles couraient	*They used to run/were running*

> **Be careful of ir verbs!**
> Only knock off the **-ons** as is the rule, not the **-issons**.

> *Example:*
> Choisir ⸱⸱⸱⸽ Nous choisiss**ons** ⸱⸱⸱⸽ choisiss ⸱⸱⸱⸽ Je choisiss**ais**
>
> **Finir** – *to finish*   (**Nous finissons**, regular present tense verb)

Je finissais	*I used to finish/was finishing*
Tu finissais	*You used to finish/were finishing*
Il finissait	*He used to finish/was finishing*
Elle finissait	*She used to finish/was finishing*
Nous finissions	*We used to finish/were finishing*
Vous finissiez	*You used to finish/were finishing*
Ils finissaient	*They used to finish/were finishing*
Elles finissaient	*They used to finish/were finishing*

The only exception is **être**. For the imperfect tense of **être**, we do not go to the **nous** form in the present tense (**nous sommes**). Instead it has an imperfect stem of **ét**, but the endings remain the same as for all other verbs.

Être – *to be*	
J'étais	*I was*
Tu étais	*You were*
Il était	*He was*
Elle était	*She was*
Nous étions	*We were*
Vous étiez	*You were*
Ils étaient	*They were*
Elles étaient	*They were*

A note on reflexive verbs

Reflexive verbs can also be used in the **imparfait**. They are treated the very same as the other groups of verbs. You go to the **nous** form of the present tense and add the appropriate ending in the **imparfait**. *The reflexive pronoun does not change.*

> *Example:* Je m'habillais *I used to get dressed/was getting dressed*
>
> Tu te levais *I got up/was getting up*
>
> Ils se couchaient *They went asleep/were going asleep*

Exercise 2

Now in the following sentences, can you change the verb in brackets to the correct form of the **imparfait**?

1 Il _____ (travailler) comme ingénieur.

2 Elle _____ (aller) à l'école à pied.

3 Ils _____ (jouer) au foot chaque samedi.

4 Vous _____ (être) voisins ?

5 Nous _____ (partir) en vacances chaque été.

6 Je _____ (faire) partie de l'équipe de foot.

7 J' _____ (aller) au cinéma.

8 Tu _____ (habiter) à Dublin ?

9 Nous _____ (lire) beaucoup.

10 C' _____ (être) chouette !

The **ce**, or *it* form is conjugated like **il** and **elle**; *it was great!*

8.3 **Some irregularities**

1 Verbs which end in **-cer** and **-ger** have minor spelling changes in the imperfect.
The only irregularities are in the **nous** and **vous** forms.

Manger – *to eat*

Je mangeais	Nous mang**ions** ❖···	⎧ The only irregularity
Tu mangeais	Vous mang**iez** ❖···	⎨ is in the **nous** and **vous**
Il mangeait	Ils mangeaient	form where we do not have
Elle mangeait	Elles mangeaient	⎩ the **e** before the **imparfait** stem.

Lancer – *to throw*

Je lançais	Nous lan**cions** ❖···	⎧ Again, just the **nous**
Tu lançais	Vous lan**ciez** ❖···	⎨ and **vous** form. There is no
Il lançait	Ils lançaient	**cédille** here.
Elle lançait	Elles lançaient	

Why does it happen?

No, it is not to create extra work for you! There is an understandable explanation.
A **g** or a **c** followed by an **a** would make a hard **g** or **c** sound, like **gave** or **cave**
in English.

When we add the **e** after the **g** and
change the **c** to **ç** we now have a softer
and easier way to pronounce words.

Like **gave** or **cave**
in English!

Like in **gel** or **cell**
in English!

2 One other little exception

Verbs whose **imparfait** stem ends in an **i** will take a **double i** in the **nous** and **vous** form of the imparfait:

> *Example:* Étudier ···⫽ nous étudi**ons** ···⫽ étudi *(stem)*

To study

So **étudier** and similar verbs (**rire** *to laugh,* **sourire** *to smile* and **vérifier** *to check*) go like this:

J'étudiais	Nous étud**iions**
Tu étudiais	Vous étud**iiez**
Il étudiait	Ils étudiaient
Elle étudiait	Elles étudiaient

3 A little point to note

Falloir *(to be necessary)* and **pleuvoir** *(to rain)* are used only in the **il** form: **il fallait** *(it was necessary)* and **il pleuvait** *(it was raining).* You don't say *I was raining!*

> ## À vos marques ! Prêts ? Partez !

Now, have you learned **par cœur** those three points above? The next exercise is a sprint test. Why not try to time yourself?

Exercise 3

Put in the correct form of the **imparfait**.

1	Lancer	Elle _____
2	Pleuvoir	Il _____
3	Étudier	Nous _____
4	Falloir	Il _____
5	Rire	Nous _____
6	Manger	Elles _____
7	Lancer	Je _____
8	Manger	tu _____
9	Sourire	Vous _____
10	Manger	Vous _____

8.4 To make a negative phrase in the imparfait

Ne comes directly before the verb and **pas** (or **jamais**, etc.) comes after the verb.
Ça y est ! You weren't expecting it to be so short, were you?

> *Example:* Il **n'**était **pas** content.   *He wasn't happy.*
>
>   Il **ne** pleuvait **pas**.   *It wasn't raining.*

Reflexive verbs and negative phrases in the imparfait

Remember in chapter 6 on **The Passé Composé** we learned about the order of words in a sentence. Let's take a little part of the rhyme here:

> **Je** before **ne** before **me** before
> **verb** before **pas**.

So if we have a reflexive verb, it follows this rule.

> *Example:*   Je ne me couchais jamais avant minuit.
> *I never used to go to bed before midnight.*

Exercise 4

Change the infinitive of the verb to the correct form of the **imparfait**.

1 Il _____ (pleuvoir) toute la journée.

2 Les garçons et les filles _____ (lancer) des boules de papier en classe.

3 Elle _____ (avoir) mal à la tête.

4 Tous les samedis, je_____ (sortir) avec mes amis.

5 Au lycée, nous _____ (étudier) l'allemand et le français.

6 Ils ne _____ _____ (se lever) pas avant 11h.

7 Mon père_____ (être) professeur.

8 Nous _____ (habiter) à Cork.

9 Tu _____ (partir) souvent en vacances.

10 Elles (ne pas pouvoir) _____ comprendre l'exercice.

> Hint: Do question number 10 as a positive expression first, e.g: Elles (pouvoir) and then fit the negative around it.

Exercise 2

Now can you say what each of the above sentences means in English?

> **À vos marques ! Prêts ? Partez !**

Exercise 5

Another race! For the next exercise you have to be quick off the mark. Before you start, make sure you are confident that you know the rules for forming verbs in the **imparfait**. Can you change the present tense verbs to the **imparfait**? You may like to change them to the infinitive first, but it's a race. Be quick!

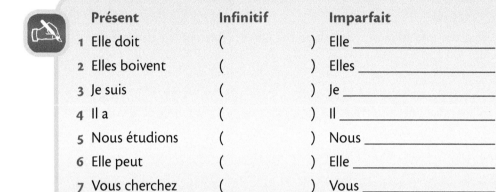

	Présent	Infinitif	Imparfait
1	Elle doit	( )	Elle _____
2	Elles boivent	( )	Elles _____
3	Je suis	( )	Je _____
4	Il a	( )	Il _____
5	Nous étudions	( )	Nous _____
6	Elle peut	( )	Elle _____
7	Vous cherchez	( )	Vous _____
8	Nous nous lavons	( )	Nous nous _____
9	Tu choisis	( )	Tu _____
10	Ils vont	( )	Ils _____

How did you do? Take a note of your time, but remember it is your accuracy that really matters. *Sprint tests* like these keep you on your toes!

The following passage describes a typical day for Lucy when she used to spend her holidays with her family beside the beach in Curracloe. Change the verb in brackets to put it in the **imparfait**.

D'habitude, je (**faire**) _____ la grasse matinée.

De temps en temps, je (**se lever**) _____ tôt et (**aller**) _____ à la plage.

Le vendredi, j'(**aller**) _____ en ville avec ma mère pour acheter des provisions.

Tous les jours, je (**nager**) _____ et mon frère et moi (**jouer**) _____ au tennis.

Le soir, mon père (**préparer**) _____ un barbecue.

8.5 The imparfait is used to indicate the following:

1 Repeated actions in the past

> *Example:*
> Quand j'étais petit, **nous allions** chez mes grands-parents chaque semaine.
> *When I was young, **we used to go** to my grandparents every week.*

2 Descriptions such as weather, time, age and feelings

> *Example:*
> | Je me sentais malade. | *I was feeling sick.* |
> | J'avais treize ans. | *I was thirteen.* |
> | Paul avait peur. | *Paul was afraid.* |

3 What used to happen over a period of time

> *Example:*
> Il allait en Espagne.
> *He went/was going to Spain.*
> ___
> J'allais en ville avec mes amis.
> *I used to go into town with my friends.*
> ___
> J'allais à l'école primaire dans mon quartier
> *I used to go to primary school in my area.*

Compare the two sentences below, the first in the **imparfait** and the second in the **passé composé**:

> | 1 Il allait en Espagne. | *He went/**was going** to Spain.* |
> | 2 Il est allé en Espagne. | *He **went** to Spain.* |

In Example 1, the English translation is 'was going', this **imparfait** is often associated with this *-ing* (was doing) in English. On the other hand, the **passé composé** in the second sentence implies that he has left and is probably there. Let's take another example:

> 1 Elle finissait ses devoirs.   *She **was finishing** her homework.*
>
> 2 Elle a fini ses devoirs.   *She **finished** her homework.*

Similar to the previous example, the *-ing*, the ***was finishing***, of the **imparfait** in the first sentence implies her homework is still ongoing, whereas the *-ed*, the ***finished***, of the **passé composé** in the second would naturally lead us to believe that her homework is completely finished and out of the way.

4   Background information when used with the passé composé/ bubble and pin theory

> 1 Je regardais la télévision quand ma tante a télephoné.
>
>   *I was watching television when my aunt phoned.*
>
> 2 J'étais en ville quand j'ai vu mon amie Claudine.
>
>   *I was in town when I saw my friend Claudine.*

Why call it the bubble and pin theory? Take a look at the first example. You are sitting there in a trance watching your favourite show or engrossed in a football match and next thing, *pop!* Your happy, trance-like state is 'burst' because of the disruption.

We can also apply this reasoning to the second example. You were in town walking along, engrossed in all the shops, thinking about what you are going to buy when you see your friend waving at you. Again, this has the effect of taking you out of your daze. There has been an interruption to the description or background. This is often indicated by the conjunction **quand**.

*The continuous action or description is in the **imparfait** and the interruption is in the **passé composé**.*

8.6 The relationship between le passé composé and the imparfait

1 To create background and action

Because they serve different, but complementary, purposes, the **imparfait** and the **passé composé** are often used in conjunction with one another. Most stories switch between description and narration. You need to describe a scene before you can say what happens in it. The **imparfait** is used to describe the scene. You need to create your stage before you allow the action to unfold.

And even when you've given some description, you still need to keep the action moving.

2 The frame and the picture

The **imparfait** describes past situations, giving the colour to the picture, while the **passé composé** gives the more obvious black and white frame.

The **imparfait** shows and gives us more detail and the **passé composé** tells the basic fact of the story.

> *Example:* J'étais à la plage quand j'ai perdu mon portefeuille.
> *I was at the beach when I lost my wallet.*

The key event? Of course, I lost my wallet (described using the **passé composé**). However, more detail to the story is that I was at the beach when I lost it (described using the **imparfait**).

Because it has no starting point or ending point, actions told in the **imparfait** *do not advance the story*. They add more information, more description about the same point of time. On the other hand, the **passé composé** is all about the movement. For example, we could move the story forward in the above example. What happened when you lost your wallet? Well, you went to the police station to report the theft:

Je suis allé au commissariat. You could then describe that same point in time in further detail. You want to say it was terrible: **C'était affreux !** Here we can blend in both the **passé composé** and the **imparfait** to complement one another.

3 It can depend on the context

It really depends on how we want to express events when deciding on whether to use the **passé composé** or the **imparfait**.

Example: Je voyageais aux États-Unis avec mes parents tous les ans.
I used to travel to America with my parents every year.

J'ai voyagé aux États-Unis avec mes parents l'année dernière.
I travelled to America with my parents last year.

So you see, sometimes we can use the same verb. Example: **voyager**, but in either the **passé composé** or the **imparfait**, depending on what you are trying to get across.

8.7 Key words and phrases to indicate either le passé composé or l'imparfait

These key words indicate the imparfait:

D'habitude	*Usually*
Le week-end	*Every weekend*
Souvent	*Often*
Tous les jours	*Every day*
En général	*In general*
Normalement	*Normally*
Le lundi	*On mondays*
Le soir	*In the evenings*
Chaque semaine, chaque mois, chaque année	*Every week, every month, every year*

Whereas these key words indicate the passé composé:

Un jour	*One day*
Lundi, mardi, etc.	*Monday, Tuesday, etc.*
Plusieurs fois	*Several times*
Une/deux fois	*Once, twice*
Un week-end	*One weekend*
Tout d'un coup	*Suddenly*

While these indicator phrases are useful, they are not always used in sentences in the past tense, but if they are, be on the alert! It can make deciding between the **passé composé** and the **imparfait** a little easier.

8.8 **Decision time!**

In this section, you will find some revision exercises that you need to attempt. Here is a final reminder of what you should ask yourself before you decide on whether you should use the **passé composé** or the **imparfait**:

You should ask yourself the following questions when deciding if it would be best to use the **passé composé** or the **imparfait**:

1 Does the *action move* the story forward in any way?

2 Is the action *limited*, within a *certain time frame*?

3 Does the action state a fact, a clear and *definite beginning and end* in the past?

---

4 Does the verb/action show the *background*? Does it describe a *state, how someone was feeling or looking*?

5 Is it our *bubble and pin theory*? Is there a continuous action, which is interrupted by another action? Remember, the continuous action is in the **imparfait** and the interruption is in the **passé composé**.

Example: Je regardais la télé quand le téléphone a sonné.

6 Can you relate it to *-ing* in English?

7 Is it a *repeated, habitual action*, something you always did?

Tip:
Use the **passé composé** in these cases.

Tip:
Use the **imparfait** in these cases.

We use the word 'action' throughout the checklists as, remember, the **passé composé** and the **imparfait** are simply verbs, when all is said and done. You might not always think you are active, but you are.

Even, **j'étais calme**, in describing how you were feeling in the past, is from **être**, *to be*, so you are *being* calm!

Revision exercises

1 **In the passage below you should**

say which tense the verb is in.

say why this is the case.

L'anniversaire de Ciara

C'était son anniversaire et **Ciara avait** seize ans. **Elle mangeait** son petit déjeuner quand **elle a décidé** d'aller en ville. Elle **bavardait** avec ses amies quand tout d'un coup, **elle a glissé** sur une peau de banane. **Son sac est tombé** sur le trottoir. **Les passants ont commencé** à rire !

Now can you create a similar **petite histoire** to describe an unfortunate event that happened during a day out?

2 **Cherchez l'intrus ! Can you find the odd one out?**

e.g. Avons ont avaient avez ····❖ avaient

1 Adore adorent adoraient adorez _____

2 Aller allait allions allaient _____

3 Était étiez été étions _____

4 Buvais buvons buvions buvait _____

5 Peut pouvait pouvons peux _____

6 Mange manges mangions mangeons _____

7 Prends prend prenons prenions _____

8 Voit voir voyions voyons vois _____

9 Partait partais partions partir _____

10 Sortais sort sortez sortons _____

3 Fill in the gaps in the following table

	Passé composé			Imparfait		
Dire	je ____	nous _____	ils ____	je ____	nous _____	ils ____
Faire	je ____	nous _____	ils ____	je ____	nous _____	ils ____
Mettre	je ____	nous _____	ils ____	je ____	nous _____	ils ____
Être	je ____	nous _____	ils ____	je ____	nous _____	ils ____
Sortir	je ____	nous _____	ils ____	je ____	nous _____	ils ____
Aller	je ____	nous _____	ils ____	je ____	nous _____	ils ____
Avoir	je ____	nous _____	ils ____	je ____	nous _____	ils ____
Prendre	je ____	nous _____	ils ____	je ____	nous _____	ils ____
Vouloir	je ____	nous _____	ils ____	je ____	nous _____	ils ____
Venir	je ____	nous _____	ils ____	je ____	nous _____	ils ____

4 Choose the correct option from the multiple choice below. Should the verb in the sentence be in the passé composé or the imparfait?

1 Nous _____ le film deux fois. a) avons vu b) voyions ◯

2 Il ne (n') _____ au concert. a) est pas allé b) allait pas ◯

3 Normalement, il _____ les poèmes par cœur. a) a su b) savait ◯

4 Mon grand-père _____ quand j'avais dix ans. a) est mort b) mourait ◯

5 J' _____ piqué par
   un moustique pendant la nuit.

   a) ai été   b) étais   ◯

6 Hier soir, à huit heures, mon voisin
   _____ chez nous.

   a) arrivait   b) est arrivé   ◯

7 Vous _____
   votre examen hier ?

   a) avez passé   b) passiez   ◯

8 Tout d'un coup il a vu le taureau
   et il _____ en courant.

   a) est parti   b) partait   ◯

9 Hier soir, je me _____
   de bonne heure.

   a) couchais   b) suis couché   ◯

10 Ma famille et moi _____ en
    train de manger, lorsque le
    téléphone a sonné.

    a) étions   b) avons été   ◯

Now that you have completed the exercise, you should check the answers with a friend. If your answers are different, you must argue your point. Why are you right?

5 **Choose whether the following verbs should be in the passé composé or the imparfait**

1 J' _____ (aller) au magasin quand je _____ (tomber).

2 Tara _____ (ne pas vouloir) faire ses devoirs hier soir.

3 Pendant les vacances nous _____ (se coucher) tard le soir.

4 Ma petite sœur _____ (avoir) un peu peur quand elle _____
   (voir) le chien.

5 Ma mère et moi _____ (regarder) la télé quand ma tante
   _____ (téléphoner).

6 Elles _____ (sortir) quand elles _____ (entendre) un bruit.

7 Comme il _____ (pleuvoir), Simon et moi _____ (aller) au cinéma.

8 Quelle horreur, la neige _____ (tomber) quand les touristes _____ (perdre) leur chemin.

9 Alors que nous _____ (aller) à Waterford, le train _____ (s'arrêter).

10 Chaque soir mes amis et moi _____ (jouer) aux jeux-vidéo.

Now you need to think back on this chapter and what you have been learning and ask yourself if you can do the following:

Récapitulez

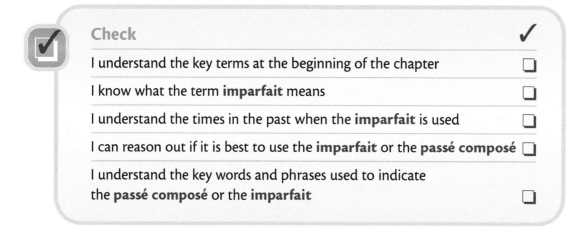

Check	✓
I understand the key terms at the beginning of the chapter	☐
I know what the term **imparfait** means	☐
I understand the times in the past when the **imparfait** is used	☐
I can reason out if it is best to use the **imparfait** or the **passé composé**	☐
I understand the key words and phrases used to indicate the **passé composé** or the **imparfait**	☐

Chapter 9
Le Futur
The Future Tense

Key words

···▷ Futur Proche/Immédiat   ···▷ Distant Future
···▷ Futur Simple   ···▷ Prediction
···▷ Near Future

9.1 A quick word

Whenever you want to talk about what you are going to do tomorrow, or anytime in the future, you need the future tense. French has two future tenses, the **futur proche** and the **futur simple** – just like in English! It's one of the easier tenses in French to understand. Don't believe me? Read on!

The **futur proche** is known as the near future because it refers to a time in the future that isn't too far away. It can also be called the **futur immédiat**.

It is made up of the present tense of **aller** plus the *infinitive* of the verb.

> *Example:* **Je vais faire mes devoirs.** *I am going to do my homework.*

It means that you are going to do your homework relatively soon in the future.

The **futur simple** or *simple future* is so called because it is simply a one-word tense. So it's simple – it has no 'helping' or auxiliary verb of **avoir** or **être**, as we had in the **passé composé**.

> *Example:*   Je ferai mes devoirs.   *I will do my homework.*

You have made the general statement that you will do
your homework … just when exactly in the future will you do it?

While in most contexts we can use either the **futur proche** or **futur simple**, there
can be a difference depending on the meaning we want to get across. In French, just
like in English, we use the two phrases *going to do something* and *will do something*.

9.2 Le futur proche

The present tense of **aller** (*to go*) is as follows:

je vais	nous allons
tu vas	vous allez
il va	ils vont
elle va	elles vont

> *Examples:*   Je vais regarder la télévision maintenant.
> *I am going to watch television now.*
>
> Elle va sortir avec ses amis.
> *She is going to go out with her friends.*
>
> Nous allons manger des frites ce soir.
> *We are going to eat chips this evening.*
>
> Ils vont aller en ville demain soir.
> *They are going to go to town tomorrow evening.*

In the last example, *they are going to go*, we use the present tense of the verb
aller followed by the infinitive of **aller**, again to create the expression
I am going to go. This is perfectly acceptable!

Exercise 1

Write these sentences in the **futur proche**.

> *Eg.* Venir : Il va venir samedi soir
>
> **1** Aller : Il _____ _____ au cinéma ce soir.
>
> **2** Lire : Vous _____ _____ le roman ?
>
> **3** Visiter : Elles _____ _____ le week-end prochain.
>
> **4** Sortir : Je _____ _____ plus tard.
>
> **5** Venir : Mes cousins _____ _____ en Irlande la
>
> semaine prochaine.

9.3 Reflexive verbs in the futur proche

> *Note:*
> The present tense of **aller**, followed by the reflexive pronoun and the infinitive of the verb!

Take a look at the full conjugation of the verb **s'amuser**, *to enjoy oneself*:

Je vais m'amuser	*I am going to enjoy myself*
Tu vas t'amuser	*You are going to enjoy yourself*
Il va s'amuser	*He is going to enjoy himself*
Elle va s'amuser	*She is going to enjoy herself*
Nous allons nous amuser	*We are going to enjoy ourselves*
Vous allez vous amuser	*You are going to enjoy yourselves*
Ils vont s'amuser	*They are going to enjoy themselves*
Elles vont s'amuser	*They are going to enjoy themselves*

The reflexive pronoun in **s'amuser** changes as usual to suit the personal pronoun; **je** with **me**, **tu** with **te**, **il** with **se**, etc.

Exercise 2

Can you translate the following?

1   I am going to get up. _____.

2   You are going to go to bed. _____.

3   He is going to get up. _____.

4   She is going to wake up. _____.

5   We are going to enjoy ourselves. _____.

9.4 To make verbs negative in the futur proche

When a conjugated verb is followed by an infinitive, the **ne** is before the conjugated verb (**aller**) and **pas** comes after it, followed by the infinitive.

> *Example:*   Nous n'allons pas sortir ce soir.
> *We are not going to go out this evening.*
>
> Je ne vais pas me lever ce matin.
> *I am not going to get up this morning.*

Exercise 3

A   Your first task is to put these sentences into the **futur proche**.

B   When you have done this, you need to make the sentence negative.

E.g. Il _____ (voyager) en France cet été ?

A   Il va voyager en France cet été.
He is going to travel in France this summer.

B   Il ne va pas voyager en France cet été.
He is not going to travel in France this summer.

1 Demain, je _____ (partir) à Paris.

2 Il _____ (nager).

3 Il _____ (pleuvoir).

4 Elle_____ (faire) du shopping.

5 Vous _____ (jouer) au tennis ?

9.5 Useful phrases of time that indicate the futur proche

The **futur proche** is used when events are going to occur soon in the future. How soon? These phrases indicate a time in the future that is not too far away, meaning that much of the time we can use the **futur proche** with them.

Ce soir	*This evening*
Dans deux semaines	*In two weeks*
Dans deux jours	*In two days*
Demain	*Tomorrow*
Demain soir	*Tomorrow evening*
Lundi, mardi, mercredi prochain	*Monday, Tuesday, next Wednesday*
La semaine prochaine	*Next week*
Le week-end prochain	*Next weekend*
Le lendemain	*The following day*
Plus tard	*Later*

Exercise 5

A Change the infinitive of the verb to the correct form of the **futur proche**:

> *E.g.* Je _____ (sortir) avec mes amis demain.
>
> *Je vais sortir avec mes amis demain.*
>
> 1 Il _____ _____ (aller) au cinéma ce soir.
> 2 Vous _____ _____ (lire) le roman demain soir ?
> 3 Elles _____ _____ _____ (se coucher) à midi.
> 4 Je _____ _____ _____ (se reposer) samedi.
> 5 Ma petite sœur _____ _____ _____
>   _____ _____ (ne pas se coucher) de bonne heure !
> 6 Nous _____ _____ _____ _____ (ne pas travailler)
>   pendant les vacances.
> 7 Tu _____ _____ (sortir) avec tes copains ?
> 8 Qu'est-ce qu'ils _____ _____ (faire) ce soir ?
> 9 Ma sœur et moi _____ _____ (rester) chez
>   mon frère à Galway.
> 10 Mes cousins _____ _____ (venir) en Irlande
>   la semaine prochaine.

B Now that the sentences are in the **futur proche**, can you say what they mean?

Les textos

Exercise 6

Amy has sent the following text to her friend Niamh.
What is the problem?

> Alan m'a téléphoné. Il va faire du baby-sitting.
> Il ne va pas aller au cinéma. Je suis furieuse !

Write Niamh's reply in French: She is going to go into town now, but she is going to ring Amy at seven o'clock this evening.

 Since his text to Amy, Alan's plans have changed. He no longer has to look after his little niece, yet he has forgotten about his plans with Amy! Write in French his text to his friend Mark. He says:

Useful phrases:
Aller en ville
Je vais te téléphoner

- He is not going babysitting.
- He is going to play football now and is going to drop by Mark's house later.

Useful phrases:
Jouer au foot
Passer chez toi

Le week-end prochain

Exercise 7

To get you through Monday morning, you are already thinking about what you are going to do next weekend.

Write 5–6 sentences to say what you and your friends are going to do.

Some ideas:

Passer chez Anna/Brian
Organiser une boum
Rendre visite à mes cousins
Aller en ville, au cinéma
Jouer au foot

9.6 **Le futur simple**

Formation of the futur simple:

Add the future tense endings to the infinitive of the verb you want to use.
The endings are all the same for **-er**, **-ir** and **-re** verbs.

The **futur simple** endings for all verbs are:
ai, as, a, ons, ez, ont

To make the future stem for **-er** and **-ir** verbs, you use the whole infinitive verb.
For **-re** verbs, though, you drop the **e**. Take a look:

-er	parler	⋯⋙	je parler**ai**		
-ir	finir	⋯⋙	je finir**ai**		
-re	vendre	⋯⋙	drop the **e**	⋯⋙	je vendr**ai**

Parler – *to speak*	**Finir** – *to finish*	**Vendre** – *to sell*
je parler**ai**	je finir**ai**	je vendr**ai**
tu parler**as**	tu finir**as**	tu vendr**as**
il/elle parler**a**	il/elle finir**a**	il/elle vendr**a**
nous parler**ons**	nous finir**ons**	nous vendr**ons**
vous parler**ez**	vous finir**ez**	vous vendr**ez**
ils/elles parler**ont**	ils/elles finir**ont**	ils/elles vendr**ont**

Dropping the **e** from **-re** verbs makes the stem easier to learn.
Have you noticed? This means the stem for all future tense verbs ends in **r**.

The key to the **futur simple** is **r**.

Exercise 8
Verb sprint:

Now can you fill in the correct parts
of the verbs in the **futur simple**?

Choisir	Je	_____	Ils	_____
Loger	tu	_____	Elle	_____
Dormir	Je	_____	Nous	_____
Préparer	Il	_____	Vous	_____
Rester	Tu	_____	Il	_____
Dormir	Elle	_____	Elles	_____
Jouer	Je	_____	Tu	_____
Vendre	Nous	_____	Vous	_____
Finir	Il	_____	Elle	_____
Attendre	Nous	_____	Vous	_____

Well done!

9.7 Irregular stems in the future

The following verbs have irregular stems in the future, but the future tense
endings do not change.

We will use the **je** form for the examples. Except of course for **pleuvoir**, which
will naturally just be used in the **il** form; **il pleuvra**, *it will rain.* Obviously you
will not be raining any time in the future!

Il faudra, *it will be necessary*, is also only used in the **il** form.

Verb	Stem that has a double *r* in the future	Le Futur	In English
courir	courr	Je courrai	*I will run*
envoyer	enverr	J'enverrai	*I will send*
pouvoir	pourr	Je pourrai	*I will be able to*
voir	verr	Je verrai	*I will see*

Verb	Stem that has *dr* in the future	Le futur	In English
falloir	faudr	Il faudra (only ever used in the **il** form)	*It will be necessary*
tenir	tiendr	Je tiendrai	*I will hold*
venir	viendr	Je viendrai	*I will come*
devenir	deviendr	Je deviendrai	*I will come back*

Verb	Other irregular stems	Le futur	In English
acheter	achèter (yes it is the full form but with an accent (`) on the first **e**!)	j'achèterai	*I will buy*
aller	ir	j'irai	*I will go*
appeler	appell	j'appellerai	*I will call*
avoir	aur	j'aurai	*I will have*
devoir	devr	je devrai	*I will have to*
être	ser	je serai	*I will be*
faire	fer	je ferai	*I will make/do*
recevoir	recevr	je recevrai	*I will receive*
savoir	saur	je saurai	*I will know*
vouloir	voudr	je voudrai	*I will like*

learn par cœur

You need to learn these irregular stems **par cœur**!

Exercise 9

As practice, write out the full form of **courir**, **recevoir** and **savoir**.

Exercise 10

Can you find the **futur simple** stems for the following irregular verbs?

Être	je _____ ai
Avoir	tu _____ as
Aller	Il _____ a
Faire	Elle _____ a
Pouvoir	Nous _____ ons
Venir	Vous _____ ez
Vouloir	Ils _____ ont
Tenir	Elles _____ ont

9.8 A checklist for the futur simple

Let's do a round-up of a few things to do with the **futur simple**:

learn par cœur

Learn the endings for the **futur simple par cœur**.

● drop the **e** from **-re** verbs.

● in the present tense, the **ils** and **elles** forms end in **ent**.
However, in the future tense, the **ils** and **elles** forms end in **-ont**.

● learn the irregular stems **par cœur**.

Exercise 11

Rewrite the following sentences, changing the present tense verb to the **futur simple**.

Tip:

Ask yourself three questions as you do this exercise:

1 Where is the verb?
2 What is the infinitive?
3 Is the stem regular or irregular in the future tense?

 Eg. Je **fais** de la natation

⋯⋗ Je ferai de la natation

1 Je suis content.

_____

2 Il pleut dans l'est.

_____

3 Tu joues au foot tous les jours.

_____

4 Mon oncle et ma tante viennent en Irlande pendant les vacances.

_____

5 Il donne l'argent à son frère.

_____

6 Elles n'arrivent pas demain.

_____

7 J'ai quatorze ans.

_____

8 Il faut rester à la maison.

_____

9 Robert et James descendent à la plage.

_____

10 Vous allez en ville ?

_____

Exercise 12
Pick n' Mix

In Ireland, we do not always have the sunniest of summers! Describe your ideal summer. What tense do you think you will use? The **futur simple** is appropriate. This is a distant event, remember; this ideal summer may never happen, but we'll see, **on verra** !

Choose from these verb and vocabulary selections.

Pick 'n' mix verbs

Je bronzerai …
Il fera …
Il ne pleuvra jamais …
Je nagerai
Nous pourrons aller …
J'achèterai …
Je jouerai/nous jouerons …
Ma famille et moi irons …

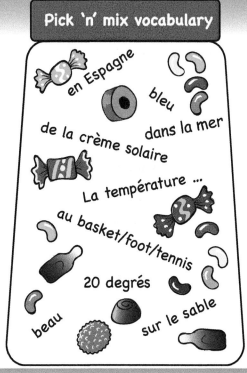

Pick 'n' mix vocabulary

en Espagne
bleu
de la crème solaire
dans la mer
La température …
au basket/foot/tennis
20 degrés
beau
sur le sable

Exercise 13

Fill in the gaps in the crossword with the correct part of the verb from the clues given below:

Across

2 **Futur simple** of pleuvoir [*il form*].

6 **Futur simple** of courir [*vous form*].

7 **Futur simple** of être [*tu form*].

8 **Futur simple** of aller [*ils form*].

9 **Futur simple** of devoir [*tu form*].

Down

1 The stem of **venir** in **futur simple**.

3 The stem of **envoyer** in **futur simple**.

4 **Futur simple** of recevoir [*il form*].

5 **Future simple** of tenir [*je form*].

7 **Future simple** of savoir [*nous form*].

9.9 Deciding between the futur proche and the futur simple

1. The time in the future

The **futur proche**, also called the **futur immédiat**, usually refers to a time in the near or immediate future. Just what is the immediate future you may ask. Take a look at the following examples:

> *Example:* Il fait beau aujourd'hui. Nous allons faire un barbecue !
> *It is fine today. We are going to have a barbecue!*

However, it is also acceptable to use the **futur simple**.

> *Example:* Nous ferons un barbecue !
> *We will have a barbecue!*

Study this timeline:

Présent	Futur Proche	Futur Simple
	A clear, definite time in the future.	Time not so definite. Hazier, time in the future, general statement about the future.

2. How the speaker sees the event in the future

Let's pretend you are ice-skating. You begin to stumble and you shout at your friend, **Je vais tomber**, or do you shout **Je tomberai**? Yes, the first one, in the **futur proche**; you are fairly certain you are going to fall and very soon!

3. Prediction

The **futur proche** is usually used in *speech* and in *informal writing*, so you will probably find you have been using it in letters, notes and postcards, before you even realised you were using the future tense. For example, in a note, you might say that you are going to go to the swimming pool,

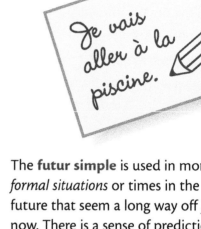

The **futur simple** is used in more *formal situations* or times in the future that seem a long way off just now. There is a sense of prediction about it. You would use it to talk about your career plans, for example. In the distant future, when you have left school, college, earned money, been on the X-Factor, you might like to be a famous singer!

Je *deviendrai chanteur/chanteuse.

The exact timeframe of when you will get your big break cannot be predicted just yet!

* **Devenir** takes the same stem as **venir** in the future; the verb *to come* has added on **de**, meaning *to become*.

The weather, as we all know, can be very difficult to predict.

Demain il pleuvra dans le sud du pays.

It will rain at some time tomorrow, but the exact hour or minute is difficult to say.

Exercise 14

Write a sentence to explain the choice of the **futur simple** in the following sentences:

- Un jour, vous aimerez l'école !
- Nous voyagerons beaucoup.
- John choisira le cadeau.
- Ils iront en vacances
- Je serai très heureux de rencontrer mes amis.

9.10 Si clauses and the futur simple

Si means *if* in French. (We will also discuss **si** clauses in chapter 10 The Conditional Tense.) The present tense follows **si**; it is the situation that is needed before the other action can take place.

Example: **Si j'ai le temps, je le ferai.**
If I have time, I will do it.

Si + present + futur simple

Only if I have the time, that is. Or we can switch it around:

Example: **Je le ferai, si j'ai le temps.**
I will do it, if I have time.

Si j'ai assez d'argent, je ferai le voyage.
If I have enough money, I will do the trip.

Or, again:
Je ferai le voyage, si j'ai assez d'argent.

What are your plans for the next few days? List five things you will do, if you have the time (**si j'ai le temps ...**) or if you have the money (**si j'ai assez de l'argent ...**).

Revision exercises

Exercise 15

Put the following verbs in the **futur proche**.

Remember the tips you have been learning along the way. In the case of negative phrases, make a positive sentence first and then sandwich the negative words correctly around it. Remember how easy it is. The verb in brackets does not change. Instead you are using the present tense of **aller**.

1 Il _____ _____ (pleuvoir) beaucoup cet hiver.

2 Elles _____ _____ (aller) en ville ce soir.

3 Elle _____ _____ _____ _____ (ne pas partir) demain.

4 Ma famille et moi _____ _____ (partir) en vacances en juin.

5 Je _____ _____ (voir) Luc la semaine prochaine.

6 Nous _____ _____ _____ _____
(ne pas sortir) le week-end prochain.

7 Ma mère _____ _____ (envoyer) des cadeaux à mon frère en Australie.

8 Vous _____ _____ (regarder) le film ce soir.

9 L'année prochaine, mes parents _____ _____ (acheter) une nouvelle maison.

10 Qu'est-ce que tu _____ _____ (faire) ?

Exercise 16

What are your plans for the future? What would you like to do when you leave school?

You are just dreaming at the moment; there is no definite timeframe, so use the **futur simple**.

Boîte de verbes

Voyager

Travailler

Devenir

Rester en Irlande

Habiter aux États-Unis

So here we are again! Now you need to think back on this chapter and what you have been learning and ask yourself if you can do the following:

Récapitulez

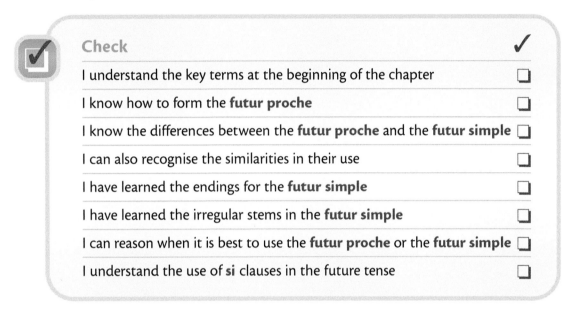

Check	✓
I understand the key terms at the beginning of the chapter	❑
I know how to form the **futur proche**	❑
I know the differences between the **futur proche** and the **futur simple**	❑
I can also recognise the similarities in their use	❑
I have learned the endings for the **futur simple**	❑
I have learned the irregular stems in the **futur simple**	❑
I can reason when it is best to use the **futur proche** or the **futur simple**	❑
I understand the use of **si** clauses in the future tense	❑

Chapter 10
Le Conditionnel
The Conditional Tense

Key words

···▷ Would/Should/Could   ···▷ Conditional clauses

···▷ Si clause   ···▷ Hypothetical

10.1 A quick word

Saturday morning. The first day of the holidays. No work to do. The sun is shining and things are looking good. What *would* you do, do you think?

Well, you might start off with this:

> Je ferais la grasse matinée.

Then you might do this:

> Je regarderais un film à la télé.

Then in the afternoon you might do this:

> Je sortirais avec mes amis.

Le conditionnel tells us what should happen or would happen. It is used to say what you would do, what he should do, where we could go, what he would love to do. It is a one word tense. You've probably used **Je voudrais** quite a lot already. Often, it is used in your textbook in the chapters on food or requesting a meal in a restaurant. The French conditional tense is really useful in everyday situations, when shopping or asking for something. It is also used to say what you would do if you had the chance.

10.2 Formation of le conditionnel

Really easy! You will see a lot of similarities in how the future and the conditional tenses are formed. There is only one set of endings for them, and most verbs – even those that are irregular in the present tense – use their infinitive as the stem.

Now, needless to say, there are a few irregular ones, but don't worry, we'll sort these out as we progress.

To form the conditional of **-er** and **-ir** verbs, add the appropriate ending to the infinitive. For **-re** verbs, drop the final **e** before adding the ending. Sound familiar? Yes, we do the same with **-re** verbs in the future tense!

The conditional tense endings are:

> **ais, ais, ait, ions, iez** and **aient**

More similarities here. These endings are exactly the same as in the **imparfait**.

Take a look:

jouer	⋯⟩	je jouerais		
finir	⋯⟩	je finirais		
vendre	⋯⟩	drop the **e**	⋯⟩	je vendrais

Donner	To give	Partir	To leave
je donner**ais**	*I would give*	je partir**ais**	*I would leave*
tu donner**ais**	*you would give*	tu partir**ais**	*you would leave*
il donner**ait**	*he would give*	il partir**ait**	*he would leave*
elle donner**ait**	*she would give*	elle partir**ait**	*she would leave*
nous donner**ions**	*we would give*	nous partir**ions**	*we would leave*
vous donner**iez**	*you would give*	vous partir**iez**	*you would leave*
ils donner**aient**	*they would give*	ils partir**aient**	*they would leave*
elles donner**aient**	*they* (fem) *would give*	elles partir**aient**	*they* (fem) *would leave*

Vendre	To sell
je vendrais	*I would sell*
tu vendrais	*you would sell*
il vendrait	*he would sell*
elle vendrait	*she would sell*
nous vendrions	*we would sell*
vous vendriez	*you would sell*
ils vendraient	*they would sell*
elles vendraient	*they* (fem) *would sell*

Lose the **e** on
-re verbs!

Rappel !

Like in the future tense, all the stems in the conditional end in **r**.

The key to **le conditionnel** is **r**.

10.3 To make a sentence negative in le conditionnel

We just need a little snippet of our rule here.
Ne before verb before **pas**.

> *Example:*
>
> | Je ne donnerais pas | *I would not give* |
> | Il ne partirait pas | *He would not leave* |

Making a negative sentence in **le présent**, **l'imparfait** and **le futur** isn't difficult. Think about what they have in common. The answer is at the end of the page. Don't look yet!*

10.4 Reflexive verbs

Just a quick reminder here. Change the verb to the conditional tense. The reflexive pronoun will not change:

> *Example:*
>
> | je m'amuserais | *I would enjoy myself* |
> | tu te coucherais | *you would go to bed* |
> | il se laverait | *he would wash himself* |
> | nous nous habillerions | *we would dress ourselves* |

10.5 Irregular stems in the conditional tense

The following verbs have irregular stems in the conditional, but the conditional tense endings do not change. Guess what? The exact same verbs are irregular in the conditional and future tenses!

We will use the **je** form for the examples. Except for **pleuvoir**, which will just be in the **il** form; **il pleuvrait**: *it would rain*. **Il faudrait** is also only used in the **il** form: *it would be necessary*.

*Answer: they are all one-word tenses, unlike the **passé composé**.

Verb	Stem	Conditional	
acheter	achèter	j'achèterais	*I would buy*
aller	ir	j'irais	*I would go*
appeler	appeller	j'appellerais	*I would call*
avoir	aur	j'aurais	*I would have*
courir	courr	je courrais	*I would run*
* devoir	devr	je devrais	*I would have to*
envoyer	enverr	j'enverrais	*I would send*
être	ser	je serais	*I would be*
faire	fer	je ferais	*I would do*
falloir	faudr	il faudrait	*it would be necessary*
pleuvoir	pleuvr	il pleuvrait	*it would rain*
pouvoir	pourr	je pourrais	*I would be able to*
recevoir	recevr	je recevrais	*I would receive*
savoir	saur	je saurais	*I would know*
tenir	tiendr	je tiendrais	*I would hold*
venir	viendr	je viendrais	*I would come*
voir	verr	je verrais	*I would see*
vouloir	voudr	je voudrais	*I would like*

*The conditional of the verb **devoir** also means *should*.

Tu devrais faire tes devoirs.	*You should do your homework.*

You've already learned these irregular stems **par cœur** in the future tense.

Let's do a quick verb workout here.
Write out the full verb for **devoir**, **pouvoir** and **tenir**.

10.6 **A checklist for le conditionnel**

Future stem +
imperfect endings
= **le conditionnel**.

Ok, let's look at what we've done to date.

- You need to learn the endings for the conditional **par cœur**.
- Remember they are the same as the **imparfait** but their stems are different, so you will still be able to work out which tense it is.
- Remember, the key for the conditional is also **r**, like the future.
- Revise the irregular stems; remember they are the same as the future tense.

Exercise 1

Write the following verbs in the conditional tense

1 Je (vouloir) _____ du thé, s'il vous plaît.

2 (Pouvoir) _____ -vous venir ici, s'il vous plaît ?

3 Mes amis et moi (vouloir) _____ partir.

4 J'(adorer) _____ aller en Italie.

5 Tu (vouloir) _____ rester chez moi ?

6 Dean (venir) _____ s'il avait le temps.

7 Les touristes n'(aimer) _____ pas aller en ville.

8 Quel (être) _____ le tarif pour le séjour ?

9 Nous (s'amuser) _____ bien !

10 Ma sœur (adorer) _____ jouer
au tennis à Wimbledon.

Exercise 2

Decide on the correct part of the verb and then fill in the crossword

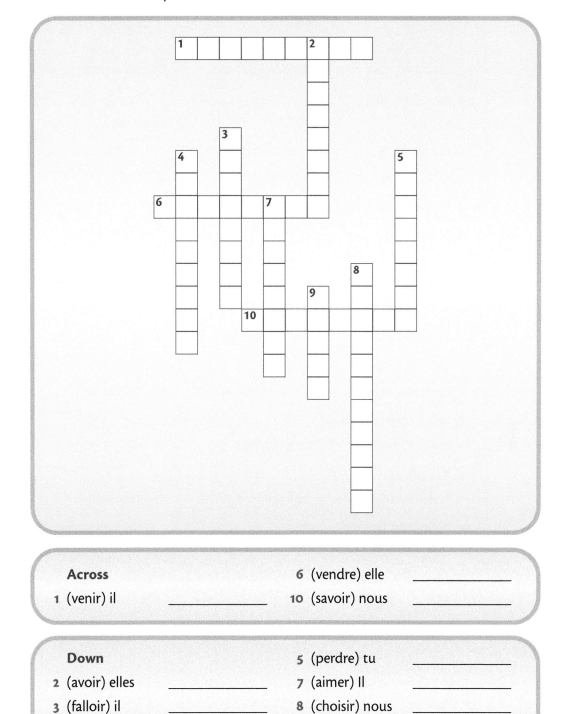

| **Across** | **6** (vendre) elle _____ |
| **1** (venir) il _____ | **10** (savoir) nous _____ |

Down	**5** (perdre) tu _____
2 (avoir) elles _____	**7** (aimer) Il _____
3 (falloir) il _____	**8** (choisir) nous _____
4 (tenir) vous _____	**9** (aller) j' _____

Exercise 3
Choose the correct phrase

1 I would eat

   a) Je mangeais b) Je mangerais c) Je mangerai ◯

2 He would go

   a) Il ira b) Il irait c) Il allait ◯

3 We would visit

   a) nous visiterions b) nous visitons c) nous visiterons ◯

4 I would play

   a) Je jouerai b) Je jouais c) Je jouerais ◯

5 They would drink

   a) Ils boiraient b) Ils boiront c) Ils boivent ◯

6 She would watch

   a) Elle regarderait b) Elle regardera c) Elle regardait ◯

7 You would listen

   a) Tu écouteras b) Tu écouterais c) Tu écoutais ◯

8 You (plural) would do

   a) Vous feriez b) Vous ferez c) Vous faisiez ◯

9 It would rain

   a) Il pleuvra b) Il pleuvait c) Il pleuvrait ◯

10 We would choose

   a) Nous choisirions b) Nous choisirons c) Nous choisissions ◯

10.7 If and the conditional tense

We can hear you already! What on earth is a hypothetical sentence? We include both terms here just so you can become familiar with how this point in grammar is described, even though the first one sounds much more approachable. Remember at the beginning when we talked about what you would do if it were the first day of the holidays? Chances are, while reading this, the holidays still seem quite a bit away as you work so hard! We are simply speculating: what you would do if … You know the phrase just imagine? Imagine if … what you would do if … what you could do.

> For **si** clauses/ hypothetical sentences

> Si j'étais ministre de l'Éducation, l'école commencerait à dix heures et finirait à une heure !

What would you do if you won the lottery?

> Hypothetically speaking…

> Si je gagnais à la loterie, j'achèterais une grande voiture et je partirais en vacances.
>
> *If I won the lottery, I would buy a big car and I would go on holidays.*

You need one verb in the imperfect and a second in the conditional. As you notice from above, they can come in either order in the sentence. The one immediately following the **si** is in the **imparfait**.

Do you remember using **si** in chapter 9, The Future Tense?

In the future tense, the present tense follows **si**; it is the situation that is needed before the other action can take place.

> Si j'ai le temps, je le ferai.   *If I have time, I will do it.*

Only if I have the time, that is. Or we can switch it around:

> Je le ferai, si j'ai le temps.   *I will do it if I have time.*

note:
Si + present + future

Let's look at the two rules together:

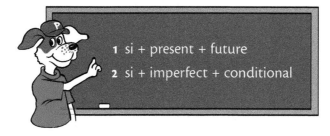

1 si + present + future
2 si + imperfect + conditional

Be careful here. As English speakers, we tend to want to use the present tense with the conditional.

Exercise 4

Can you explain the following sentences in English? Be careful of the tenses!

1 Si je vais en ville, je rencontrerai mes amis.
2 Si tu te couchais tôt, tu te lèverais tôt !
3 Mes parents viendraient avec moi, s'ils n'étaient pas obligés de travailler.
4 Si c'était dimanche aujourd'hui, j'irais me promener au parc.
5 Nous irons à la plage, s'il fait beau.

Exercise 5
Si clauses and the conditional tense

Write the correct form of the verb in the following sentences. Remember, the **si** clause will take the imperfect. The **si** clause is dependent on the conditional clause to make sense. Take a look at the following example:

> *Example:* S'il (faire) beau, j'(aller) à la plage avec mes amis.
>
> S'il faisait beau, j'irais à la plage avec mes amis.
> *If it was fine, I would go to the beach with my friends.*

S'il faisait beau, *if it was fine*, is not a full sentence. It does not quite make sense by itself. It needs further explanation. When we add **j'irais à la plage avec mes amis**, we have the full story of the sentence.

1 Si j'(être)_____ plus riche,
   j'(acheter)_____ une Ferrari.
2 Elle (aller) _____ au cinéma,
   si elle (finir)_____ ses devoirs.
3 Si mes parents (avoir) _____ le temps,
   ils (sortir) _____ le week-end.
4 Il (jouer) _____ au tennis, s'il (avoir) _____
   une raquette.
5 Maman (être) _____ ravie, si mon frère (ranger)
   _____ sa chambre.

Exercise 6
Un monde à part

If you were to live in France for a while, what would you do? Think of some of the typical things associated with the French way of life and come up with some things you would do. Using the following vocabulary hints, choose suitable verbs to make full sentences.

Brainstorm some verbs first!

Si je vivais en France …

beaucoup de croissants

… le français

… du café au lait

… mes cousins en Provence (if I had the time)

… à la plage (if it didn't rain!)

… au foot pour l'équipe de Lyon

… les magasins (if I had money)

passer un séjour à la mer

… les émissions de TV5 (if it were possible)

Revision exercises

Exercise 1
Les textos

Remember Alan and Amy in the last chapter? Well, Alan has decided he wants to stay in Amy's good books. Write the text which Alan sends to Amy.

He says sorry first of all. Then he says he would be delighted if she was able go to the cinema (remember! imparfait).

Now write Amy's reply, saying that she doesn't know.

She will go to the beach with Niamh if it is not raining.

Useful phrases:
… désolé
Je serais ravi …
Je ne sais pas …

Exercise 2
Un petit mot

Leave a note in French for your mother. You are hoping she will be impressed when she reads it and will let you go out.

Say that you would like to go to your friend's house. Say you would be happy if she is ok with that. You could help with the housework tomorrow?

(Don't forget to thank her!)

> *Useful phrases:*
> aller chez …
> tu es d'accord …
> aider

Now, let's review! Think back and answer truthfully.
If you need to check a point again, do.

Récapitulez

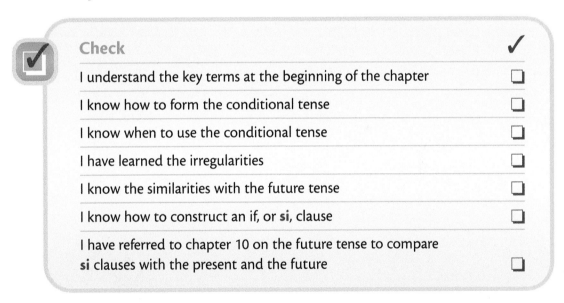

Check	✓
I understand the key terms at the beginning of the chapter	☐
I know how to form the conditional tense	☐
I know when to use the conditional tense	☐
I have learned the irregularities	☐
I know the similarities with the future tense	☐
I know how to construct an if, or **si**, clause	☐
I have referred to chapter 10 on the future tense to compare **si** clauses with the present and the future	☐

Chapter 11
Les Pronoms
Pronouns

Key words

···⋗ Personal pronouns   ···⋗ Object

···⋗ 1st, 2nd, 3rd person singular   ···⋗ Direct object

···⋗ 1st, 2nd, 3rd person plural   ···⋗ Indirect object

···⋗ Subject   ···⋗ Interrogative

11.1 A quick word

There are many types of pronouns, the most basic being subject pronouns.

The list includes others such as: object pronouns, possessive pronouns and reflexive pronouns. Remember in some chapters we talk about the importance of good foundations and piecing it all together brick-by-brick? Well, this is the same. Gradually, you will work your way through all sections, but each one will help you with the next.

The definition you probably learned in primary school still stands.

> **A pronoun takes the place of a noun. It is worth keeping the basics in mind at all times.**

11.2 Subject pronouns

Je, **tu**, **il**, **elle**, **nous**, **vous**, **ils** and **elles** are personal pronouns. At the moment, you need to know they take the place of a person's name in a sentence. We can also call them subject pronouns.

> Once students learn these subject pronouns, they're quite happy. No stress so far at all!

Then just as they get confident, they come across a sentence like this:

> Marc (habiter) à Kilkenny.

You have to change the verb to suit the noun, Marc. What do you do? If we wanted to say a person's name, e.g. Marc instead of **il**, meaning Marc lives, we would simply use the same verb ending as we would use for **il**. Take a look:

Il (habiter) à Kilkenny	⋯⋗	Il habite à Kilkenny *He lives in Kilkenny*

Don't be thrown by the use of the name (the noun) instead of the pronoun!

Marc (habiter) à Kilkenny	⋯⋗	Marc habite à Kilkenny *Marc lives in Kilkenny.*

Or this is usually the trickier one:
Ciara et Niamh (habiter) à Carlow.
Here we use the same verb ending as we would for **elles**. Remember this is for feminine plural nouns and here we have two girls. Take a look again:

Elles (habiter) à Carlow	⋯⋗	Elles habitent à Carlow *They live in Carlow.*
Ciara et Niamh (habiter) à Carlow	⋯⋗	Ciara et Niamh habitent à Carlow *Ciara and Niamh live in Carlow.*

If you have already studied the chapter on the present tense, this table will look familiar:

Pronoun (Taking the place of someone's name)		Noun	Verb – Parler (to speak)
Je	*I*	Your name (this can be called the 1st person singular)	parle
Tu	*You*	Your friend's name (you guessed it! 2nd person singular)	parles
Il	*He*	Paul (3rd person singular)	parle
Elle	*She*	Sinéad (3rd person singular)	parle
Nous	*We*	Shane and I (Careful! 1st person plural)	parlons
Vous (more than one person or to show respect, to be polite)	*You*	Nicole and Luke/Your teacher (2nd person plural)	parlez
Ils (masculine or a group of males and females)	*They*	Noel and Colm *or* Noel, Colm and Orla (3rd person plural)	parlent
Elles (female)	*They*	Ciara and Olivia (3rd person plural)	parlent

Exercise 1

Pronoun sprint: Now let's apply the rules to some practical work. Fill in the following table with the correct part of the verb. Make sure to quickly revise the verbs you need to know first!

Pronoun/nouns	Verb: Être	Donner	Aller	Avoir	Devoir	Faire	Boire
Je							
Tu							
Marc							
Nicola							
Mes amis et moi							
Vous							
Paul, Anna et Simon							
Elles							

11.3 The French pronoun on

In English we tend to think that to use the subject pronoun *one* is very posh! 'One goes to the shop' sounds a bit strange in English. However, it is almost the opposite in French. In French, **on** means *one*, *we* or people in general. It is quite informal and is used a lot, particularly in spoken French about friends and family. **On**, which you may have noticed from your textbook, fits in with **il** and **elle** as the 3rd person singular. While it can mean *one does* or *one goes*, etc., it is most often used to replaces **nous**, the first person plural, when talking about friends and family.

11.4 Tips for finding the subject and object of a sentence

Let's go back to the basics again and clarify just what exactly are subjects and objects.

> To find the subject or object of a sentence, ask yourself:
>
> 1 Where is the verb, the action word?
>
> 2 Who does the action of the verb? This is the subject.
>
> 3 What does the subject do? And to what?
>   This is the object, it receives the action.

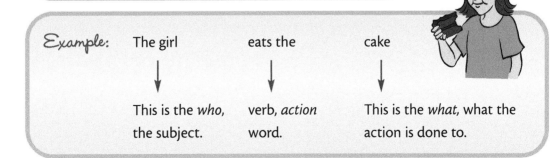

Example:

The girl	eats the	cake
↓	↓	↓
This is the *who*, the subject.	verb, *action* word.	This is the *what*, what the action is done to.

11.5 Direct object pronoun

Again, pronouns take the place of a noun, the name of somebody or something.
They will always replace somebody or something that has been spoken of already.

A direct object pronoun is used when the action is done directly to the
person or thing.

> *Example:*   Instead of, *I see Tara*, we could say, *I see her*.
>
> Instead of, *she bought a bag*, we might say, *she bought it*.

The direct object pronouns are:

me	*me*
te	*you*
le	*him/it*
la	*her/it*
nous	*us*
vous	*you*
les	*them*

Note:
If the word starts with a
vowel or a silent *h* we shorten
me, te, le and **la** to **m', t'** and
l'. Nous, vous and **les** are
never shortened.

Take a look at some examples.

> **Q** Est-ce que Caoimhe lit le roman ?   *Is Caoimhe reading the novel?*
> **A** Oui, Caoimhe le lit.   *Yes, Caoimhe is reading it.*
> **Le** replaces a masculine singular noun.

> **Q** Est-ce que Simon déteste la musique pop ?   *Does Simon hate pop music?*
> **A** Oui, il la déteste.   *Yes, he hates it.*
> **La** replaces a feminine singular noun.

> Le prof écoute les élèves.   *The teacher listens to the students.*
> Le prof les écoute.   *The teacher listens to them.*
> **Les** replace any plural noun.

Did you notice where the pronoun is placed? Right in front of the verb.
In English, pronouns come directly after the verb.

Exercise 2

Replace the underlined words by **me, te, le, la, l', nous, vous** or **les**

E.g. Elle fait *le ménage*.

Elle le fait.

1 Je ferme <u>la porte</u>.

2 Nous mangeons <u>les sandwiches</u>.

3 Ma mère invite <u>les voisins</u> à venir dîner.

4 Est-ce que vous connaissez <u>Tony et Sarah</u> ?

5 Nous apprenons <u>les langues</u>.

6 Mon frère adore <u>les frites</u>.

7 Mes cousins prennent <u>le train</u> pour aller chez nous.

8 Ma mère attend <u>ma sœur et moi</u> devant le lycée.

9 Mon père enseigne <u>la biologie</u>.

10 Tout le monde achète <u>la Nintendo Wii</u>.

11.6 Indirect object pronouns

An indirect object pronoun is used when the action is done indirectly to the object,
e.g. *I am giving the present to Peter*, or in French, **Je donne le cadeau à Peter**.
They are usually preceded by a preposition such as: *of, from, to*.

The indirect object pronouns are:

Me and te are shortened to m'
and t' before a vowel or silent h.
Lui, nous, vous and leur are
never shortened.

me	*to me*
te	*to you*
lui	*to him*
lui	*to her*
nous	*to us*
vous	*to you*
leur	*to them*

While most of the indirect object forms are the same as the direct object forms, they
have different meanings here, usually because they are translated as *to me, for me, etc.*

J'offre un cadeau à mon ami

The word *to* is implied to link the action and the object, in this case the giving of a present.

The present just doesn't magically get to your friend from the shop, you have to give it to her, bridge the gap, as it were!

Make sure to ask yourself if *me, you, him, her, us* or *them* in English might mean *to me, to you, to him, to her, to us, to them*. In English, the link word of *to* is sometimes understood and not said. Take, for example, the case of *to telephone*. We say I telephone my parents, but what we mean is I telephone to them. The link has to be made between my phoning and them.

Logically this makes sense. We don't actually phone our parents, we use a telephone or a mobile to get through to them.

Some of the main verbs we will use with indirect object pronouns are:

demander à	*to ask someone (for)*
donner à	*to give to someone*
dire à	*to say to someone*
envoyer à	*to send to someone*
expliquer à	*to explain to someone*
interdire à	*to forbid someone to*
montrer à	*to show to someone*
offrir à	*to offer to someone*
parler à	*to speak to someone*
prêter à	*to lend to someone*
ressembler à	*to look like someone*
répondre à	*to reply to someone*
téléphoner à	*to telephone (to) someone*

When you look up these verbs in your dictionary, you will usually see that the preposition is used and explained in the English translation.

learn par cœur

You should learn these verbs by heart.

Exercise 3

Replace the words underlined with an indirect object pronoun, **me**, **te**, **lui**, **nous**, **vous**, **leur**. Take care to place the indirect pronoun in the correct position in the sentence, before the verb!

1 J'enverrai <u>un email</u> à ma sœur en Australie ce soir.
2 Le soir, je donne un coup de main <u>à mes parents</u>.
3 Sinéad téléphonera <u>à ses parents</u> ce soir.
4 Marc offre des fleurs <u>à Amy</u>.
5 Elle parle <u>à ses grands-parents</u> tous les jours.
6 Le capitaine de l'équipe de foot explique les règles <u>aux joueurs</u>.
7 L'enfant montre son dessin <u>à sa mère</u>.
8 Je dis <u>à Julie</u> de venir avec nous.
9 Il ressemble <u>à son frère</u>.
10 Son père interdit <u>à Sean</u> de sortir le week-end.

11.7 Making sentences with an object (direct/indirect) pronoun negative

Now we have the object pronoun directly in front of the verb, we have to move **ne** to the the left to make room for the pronoun. **Pas** is still placed after the verb.

Montrez-moi !

Je téléphone à mon amie Suzanne le week-end.
I phone Suzanne at the weekends.

Let's do that with an indirect object pronoun and say:
I phone her at the weekends.
Je lui téléphone le week-end.

And now in a negative:
Je ne lui téléphone pas le week-end.
I don't phone her at the weekends.

11.8 Position of pronouns

(Refer back to the chapter on the **passé composé**, page 106. Order is important, for more on the position of pronouns).

Here we have our song again. **Je** before **ne** before **me** before **le** before **lui** before verb before **pas**. This little tune is getting a bit bigger! Remember we are just saying the first word on the list, but **je** is representative of **tu**, **il**, **elle**, **nous**, etc.

Chantons !

Exercise 4

Replace the groups of words underlined by either direct or indirect object pronouns. Sometimes you will need two pronouns. Remember the order!

1 Il donne <u>les devoirs</u> <u>à son professeur</u>.
2 Mon père montre <u>la carte</u> <u>à ma mère</u>.
3 Ma tante donne <u>sa voiture</u> <u>à ma sœur</u>.
4 Les parents permettent <u>aux enfants</u> de sortir.
5 Nous envoyons <u>les lettres</u> <u>à nos voisins</u>.
6 Susie montre <u>ses nouveaux vêtements</u> <u>à ses amies</u>.
7 Ma grand-mère donne souvent <u>des cadeaux</u> <u>à ma sœur et moi</u>.
8 Jack parle <u>à Luke</u> en classe.
9 Il achète un cadeau <u>pour Sophie</u>.
10 J'offre <u>un bracelet</u> <u>à ma sœur</u> pour son anniversaire.

Exercise 5

Now that's done, your next task is to make the sentences negative. Keep singing the song to yourself, or aloud, to help you!

The direct object pronoun comes before the first part of the verb in the **passé composé**.

11.9 **Pronouns and the passé composé**

Agreement with nouns and objects in the passé composé

Direct Object Pronouns

When a direct object pronoun comes before the verb **avoir** in the **passé composé**, the past participle must agree with the object.

Example: Où as-tu acheté les fleurs ?   *Where did you buy the flowers?*

Je les ai achetées au marché.   *I bought them in the market.*

Je **les** ai achet**ées** au marché.   *I bought them in the market.*

direct object   **achetées**, add an **e** and an **s**

pronoun, **les** taking – because **fleurs** is feminine plural – the place of **fleurs**

Here we know **lui** stands for Mrs. Byrne. We know if **lui** stands for a boy or girl, man or woman from what has come before in the sentence or story.

Let's take an example with a direct and indirect object pronoun:

Nous avons donné les lettres à Mme Byrne.
We have given the letters to Mrs Byrne.

Nous les lui avons donn**ées**.
We have given them to her.

Again here, we have an extra **e** because **lettre** is feminine.

Ok, let's dismantle the last example even more.

We gave them (*the letters*) making them the object of the sentence. We gave them to Mrs. Byrne, making Mrs. Byrne the indirect object of the sentence.

The past participle of a verb using **avoir** as a helping or auxiliary verb agrees in gender (feminine in the example above, so you add an 'e') and number (plural, so you can add an 's') if and only if the direct object comes before the verb. Now, we need to do this, keeping in mind the correct order and agreement if necessary.

In the **passé composé**, the indirect object also comes before the auxiliary or helping verb of **avoir**, but the past participle does not agree with them.

Don't forget the position of pronouns in the **passé composé** ! **Je** before **ne** before **me** before **le** before **lui** before **verb** before **pas**. *Before verb* refers to the helping verb of **avoir** or **être**. The **pas** will come after this.

> *Example:*
>
> | | |
> |---|---|
> | Elle a fermé la fenêtre. | *She closed the window.* |
> | Elle l'a fermée. | *She closed it.* |
> | Elle ne l'a pas fermée. | *She did not close it.* |

Exercise 6

Keeping in mind the rules above for agreement with nouns and objects in the **passé composé**, replace the words underlined with suitable pronouns. Sometimes you will need both a direct and an indirect object pronoun.

1 Paul a mangé <u>le dîner</u>.
2 Elle a pris <u>mes chaussures</u>.
3 Tu as mis <u>les lettres</u> à la poste ?
4 Elles ont fini <u>les devoirs</u>.
5 J'ai montré <u>mes photos</u> <u>à mes amis</u>.
6 Il a envoyé le message <u>à sa petite amie</u>.
7 Tu as demandé <u>à Anna et Stephen</u> ?
8 Nous avons mangé <u>la tarte aux fraises</u>.
9 Le serveur a apporté <u>un café</u> <u>à ma mère</u>.
10 Elles ont fini <u>leur travail</u>.

Exercise 7

Here we go again! Now can you make these sentences negative?

11.10 A quick word about the futur proche

In the **futur proche**, the direct object comes before the verb in the infinitive.

> *Example:*
> | | |
> |---|---|
> | Je vais regarder la télé. | *I am going to watch the television.* |
> | Je vais la regarder. | *I am going to watch it.* |
> | Elle va acheter les livres. | *She is going to buy the books.* |
> | Elle va les acheter. | *She is going to buy them.* |

11.11 The pronouns Y and En

Y used as a pronoun means *there, in it, on it, to it, at it* and replaces the name of a thing, but never a person. Y can also replace **à** + a noun that is not a person.

> *Example:*
> | | |
> |---|---|
> | Je vais au magasin. | *I'm going to the shop.* |
> | J'y vais. | *I'm going there.* |
> | Nous sommes allés au match de rugby. | *We went to a rugby match.* |
> | Nous y sommes allés. | *We went there.* |

Exercise 8
Replace the words underlined by **y**.

1 Il va <u>au cinéma</u>.
2 Je suis <u>à Dublin</u>.
3 Ils sont allés <u>au match de foot</u>.
4 Vous pensez <u>à votre voyage</u> ?
5 Il était <u>à la maison</u>.
6 Je m'intéresse <u>au sport</u>.
7 Elle va <u>à l'école</u>.
8 Mes amis et moi allons souvent <u>au cinéma</u>.
9 Tu habites <u>à Cork</u>.
10 Ils jouent souvent <u>au hurling</u>.

> Remember **y** is also found in the expression **Il y a**, *there is* or *there are*.

En as a pronoun means *some, any, of it, of them*. It replaces the partitive article: **de, du, de la**, or **des** and the indefinite article, **un, une, des** and a noun. If you see a phrase like **beaucoup de** in a sentence or a number, **en** replaces the noun. The number, or **beaucoup**, is placed at the end of the sentence.

> *Example:*
>
> | Avez-vous beaucoup de livres ? | *Do you have a lot of books?* |
> | Oui, j'en ai beaucoup. | *Yes, I have a lot of them.* |
> | Je voudrais deux cafés. | *I would like two coffees.* |
> | J'en voudrais deux. | *I want two of them.* |

Exercise 9
Replace the words underlined by **en**:

1 Nous mangeons <u>des croissants</u>.

2 J'ai assez <u>de livres</u>.

3 Il n'y a pas beaucoup <u>de chocolat</u>.

4 Ils ont mangé <u>du gâteau</u>.

5 Mon père a besoin <u>d'une nouvelle voiture</u>.

6 Il y a beaucoup <u>de pièces</u>.

7 Il a envie <u>de pain</u>.

8 Tu as peur <u>des chiens</u>.

9 Je voudrais <u>du pâté</u> s'il vous plaît.

10 Elles ont acheté beaucoup <u>de CD</u>.

11.12 **More on the order of pronouns in a sentence**

Let's add in the last bit of the puzzle! All together now!

And that is it!

> **Je** before **ne** before **me** before **le** before **lui** before **y** before **en** before verb before **pas**.

Let's look at a few examples of them used together.

Elle ne voulait pas donner sa jupe à sa sœur.	*She did not want to give her skirt to her sister.*
Elle ne voulait pas la lui donner.	*She did not want to give it to her.*
Je rencontre mes amis en ville.	*I meet my friends in town.*
Je les y rencontre.	*I meet them there.*
Il prête son portable à sa sœur.	*He is lending his mobile to his sister.*
Il le lui prête.	*He is lending it to her.*

Exercise 10
Replace the groups of underlined words by suitable pronouns.

1 Ils vendent <u>leur maison</u> <u>à ma famille</u>.
2 Je n'ai pas donné <u>le cadeau</u> <u>à mon frère</u>.
3 J'ai dit <u>la vérité</u> <u>à mes parents</u>.
4 Les élèves pensent <u>à leurs examens</u>.
5 Simone achète <u>deux romans</u> par mois.
6 J'ai assez <u>de vin</u>.
7 Ma mère interdit <u>à ma sœur et moi</u> de sortir.
8 Elle écrit souvent <u>à mon frère et moi</u>.
9 Ma sœur achète <u>beaucoup de souvenirs</u> à Nice.
10 Tara rencontrait <u>ses amis</u> <u>au cinéma</u>.

Rappel !
y before en

11.13 Les pronoms interrogatifs, lequel/interrogative pronouns, which one

An interrogative pronoun asks the question which one/what one/ which ones etc. They agree in number and gender with word they replace. They show that there is a choice or an alternative. Imagine, for example, you are in a restaurant or at a deli counter, and the waiter or assistant is asking you which dish you want.

Masculine singular	Feminine Singular	Masculine Plural	Feminine Plural
lequel	laquelle	lesquels	lesquelles

Lequel replaces **quel** + a noun

Regarde ces trois plâts.
Lequel veux-tu ?

Here **lequel**, which is masculine singular, refers to which meal you want.

Je voudrais la pomme   *I would like an apple*
Laquelle ?   *Which one?*

Exercise 11

Find the right form of **lequel** for each of these sentences.

1 Je veux la banane.
   (fem, which one)   _____ ?

2 J'aime les deux robes.
   (fem, which one)   _____ choisirais-tu ?

3 Je connais ta sœur.
   (fem, which one)   _____ ?

4 Je vois deux hommes.
   (masc, which one)   _____ est ton père ?

5 Tu as le choix entre les chocolats noirs et les chocolats au lait.
   (masc plural, which ones)   _____ veux-tu ?

6 Il y a beaucoup de filles ici.
   (fem, which one)   _____ est ta sœur ?

7 J'ai parlé à tes professeurs.
   (masc plural, which ones)   _____ ?

8 Voici deux magazines.
   (masc, which one)   _____ veux-tu ?

9 Mais il y a beaucoup de pizzas !
   (masc, which one)   _____ veux-tu ?

10 Peux-tu me donner un cd ?
   Bien sûr. (masc, which one)   _____ veux-tu ?

Now, let's review so far.

Récapitulez

Check	✓
I understand 1st, 2nd, 3rd person singular	❑
I understand 1st, 2nd, 3rd person plural	❑
I am quite clear about what the subject of a sentence is	❑
I understand what the object is	❑
I know what a direct action is	❑
I also know what indirect actions are	❑
I know the main verbs associated with indirect actions	❑
I understand agreement with **avoir** in the **passé composé**	❑
I understand the order of pronouns with the **futur proche**	❑
I have learned and understand when **y** is used	❑
I have also learned **en**	❑

Chapter 12
La Négation
Negation

Key words

···> Ne ... pas
···> One-verb tense
···> Negative phrases

···> Two-verb tense
···> Indefinite articles
···> Partitive articles

12.1 A quick word

So it's all happening with grammar. You know how to make things work, say what you are doing, where you are going. You know how to say you're happy, you love the subjects you study and you like chocolate. All the important things! Now, you need to know how to say you're not happy, the subjects you don't study and, by the way, you actually don't like chocolate. That's right, we are talking about making sentences *negative* in French. The following two little words are the key to this chapter:

12.2 Making sentences negative

Let's clarify how you make negative sentences:

> **To make a sentence *negative* in French, you put ne before the verb and pas after it.**

> *Example:*   J'aime la musique.   I like music.
>   Je n'aime pas la musique.   I don't like music.

Je regarde la télé.	⋯⋗	*I watch television.*
Je ne regarde pas la télé.	⋯⋗	*I am not watching television.*
J'aime le gaélique.	⋯⋗	*I like Irish.*
Je n'aime pas le gaélique.	⋯⋗	*I don't like Irish.*
J'aime le chocolat.	⋯⋗	*I like chocolate*
Je n'aime pas le chocolat.	⋯⋗	*I don't like chocolate.*

12.3 Using negatives with the present tense and other one-verb tenses

You've probably worked this out from the examples. Let's just make sure. In tenses such as the present, future and conditional tenses, the **ne** goes before the verb and the negative **pas** goes after it. When **ne** comes before a vowel or a silent *h*, it changes to **n'**. Think of it like a sandwich!

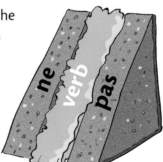

Exercise 1

Let's do a few exercises. They shouldn't take you too long. The verbs are all in the present tense. Firstly, to make it really clear, you should *underline* the verb in the sentence. Remember, **ne** before the verb and **pas** after it for the negative:

Eg. Il regarde le film   Il ne regarde pas le film.

1 J'aime le foot.   _____

2 Nous regardons la télé.   _____

3 Elles habitent à Dublin.   _____

4 Ils aiment le rugby.   _____

5 Niall prépare le dîner.   _____

6 Jessie étudie la géographie.   _____

7 Suzanne aime le français.   _____

8 Je regarde le match de foot.   _____

9 Nous prenons le car scolaire.   _____

10 L'exercice est pour lundi.   _____

12.4 Other useful negatives

Once you understand **ne** and **pas** you can use just about any other negative phrase in the same way. You will soon come across another few negative words on your travels:

1 Ne … aucun/aucune, *not any*, this negative phrase has a masculine and feminine form, but remains in the singular at all times.

Il n'y a aucun magasin près de chez moi.   *There are no shops near my house.*

Aucune is the femine form,

Example: Je ne vois aucune voiture.   *I don't see any cars.*

2 Ne … guère   *hardly*
Je ne mange guère de bonbons.   *I hardly ever eat sweets.*

3 Ne … jamais   *never*
Nous ne sortons jamais pendant la semaine.   *We never go out during the week.*

4 Ne … ni … ni   *neither … nor*
Je n'ai vu ni Joe ni Andrew en ville.   *I saw neither Joe nor Andrew in town.*

This negative phrase is very flexible!
Watch it move.

We can change it around to say, **ni mon oncle ni ma tante ne sont venus**.
Neither my uncle nor my aunt came.

This **ne … ni … ni** phrase does not take **pas**, so resist the temptation to put it in!

5 | Ne … pas du tout | not at all
Je n'aime pas du tout le fromage. | I don't like cheese at all.

6 | ne … pas encore | not yet
Il n'est pas encore arrivé. | He hasn't yet arrived.

7 | Ne … pas toujours | not always
Je ne mange pas toujours à la cantine. | I don't always eat in the canteen.

8 | Ne … personne | no one/anybody
Je n'ai vu personne. | I saw no one/I didn't see anybody

9 | Ne … plus | no more, not anymore
Elle ne joue plus au foot. | She no longer plays football.

10 | Ne … que | only
Il n'y a que deux filles ici. | There are only two girls here.

learn par cœur

As with **ne** and **pas**, **ne** is put in front of the verb and the negative word, **personne**, **que**, etc., comes after it. **Ne** is also shortened to **n'** if the verb begins with a vowel or silent h.

Yes, you need to learn these by heart. Can you say all ten in five seconds? Treat it like a tongue twister and see if you can rattle them off!

10 negatives phrases ÷ by 2 = 5 seconds

12.5 Negatives with a two-verb tense

*(Make sure to look at the chapter on the **passé composé** where we also talk about this point)*

The rule to learn

Same, same! You follow the rule, which is applied to the present tense, i.e. **ne** comes before the first part of the verb and the negative word, **pas**, for example, comes after it. The two-verb tense you will use most often is the **passé composé**.

In the **passé composé**, the first part of the verb is of course the helping verb of **avoir** or **être**.

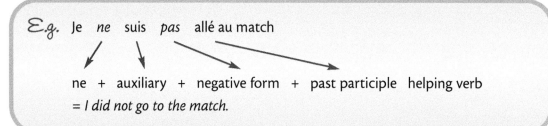

E.g. Je *ne* suis *pas* allé au match

ne + auxiliary + negative form + past participle helping verb
= *I did not go to the match.*

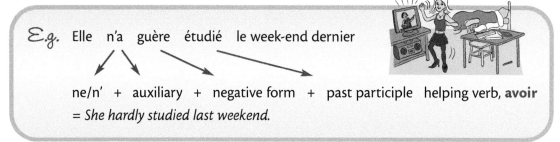

E.g. Elle n'a guère étudié le week-end dernier

ne/n' + auxiliary + negative form + past participle helping verb, **avoir**
= *She hardly studied last weekend.*

The other tense with two verbs you will come across is the **futur proche**:

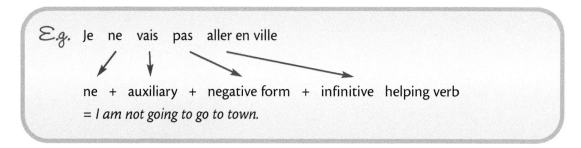

E.g. Je ne vais pas aller en ville

ne + auxiliary + negative form + infinitive helping verb
= *I am not going to go to town.*

Sorry, we do have some exceptions for these two-verb tenses!
In the case of **ne ... aucun/aucune**, **ne ... nulle part**, **ne ... personne**,
ne ... que, the second part goes after the past participle.

Example: Je n'ai vu personne.   *I saw no one.*

Il n'a vu son chien nulle part.   *He didn't see his dog anywhere.*

Je n'ai rencontré aucun copain en ville *I didn't meet any friend in town*

> For **ne ... nulle part,**
> the **nulle part** goes to the
> end of the sentence.

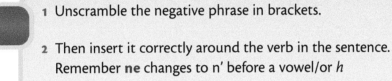

Exercise 2

The following exercise will test you on the negative phrases.
The verbs are in both the *present tense* and the **passé composé**.
Be careful of where you place the negatives in the sentences.

> Remember the
> changes to n' before a
> vowel or silent h!

1 Unscramble the negative phrase in brackets.

2 Then insert it correctly around the verb in the sentence.
   Remember **ne** changes to n' before a vowel/or *h*

a Nous avons cinq euros.   (nqeue)   _____

_____

b Nous avons étudié la semaine dernière. (gneurèe)   _____

_____

c Je vois Marie et Séan au café.   (ninien)   _____

_____

d Nous sommes allés en France.   (jneaamis)   _____

_____

e Vous habitez à Cork ?   (ulpnes)   _____

_____

f Ils aiment les frites.   (totuudsapen) _____

_____

g Elle est prête.   (cnorpenesae) _____

_____

h J'ai lu le roman hier soir.   (pasen)   _____

_____

i Il a un frère.   (qneeu)   _____

_____

j Elle a vu son amie.   (npllnueatre)   _____

_____

Exercise 3

Not quite finished! Now, can you say what the negative sentences mean in English?

12.6 Indefinite and partitive articles and the negative

(Refer back to the chapter on Articles and Nouns to revise this point)

Remember those *indefinite* and *partitive articles* we talked about?
Do you remember what happens to **un**, **une**, **des** and **du**, **de la**, **de l'** and **de** in the negative? After **ne … pas**, **ne … jamais** and **ne … plus**, a simpler form of **du/de la/de l'/des** is used. It is one simple little word, **de**, or **d'** before a vowel. Its meaning is best explained as *any* in English.

> **Ne … pas, ne jamais** and **ne … plus** are the negatives you will probably use most often!

Example: Je bois du café/Je ne bois pas **de** café.
I drink/I don't drink coffee.

Tu manges du pain ? Je ne mange pas **de** pain.
Do you eat bread?/I don't eat bread.

J'ai de l'argent/Je n'ai pas **d'**argent.
I have money/I don't have money.

J'ai une pomme/Je n'ai pas **de** pomme.
I have an apple/I don't have an apple/any apples.

J'ai un chien/Je n'ai pas **de** chien.
I have a dog/I do not have a dog.

Je mange des tomates/Je ne mange jamais **de** tomates.
I eat tomatoes/I never eat tomatoes.

Revision exercises

Exercise 1

You need to use either **ne pas**, **ne plus** or **ne jamais** to make the following sentences negative:

Ne pas, ne plus or **ne jamais** will all make sense in the following exercise.
Make the sentence negative using at least one of the negative phrases.
When you have done that, can you say what the sentences mean?

1 Les enfants mangent des bonbons.

_____

_____

2 Il reste du gâteau.

_____

_____

3 Nous prenons des cours de danse.

_____

_____

4 Dans mon école, il y a une piscine.

_____

_____

5 Le matin, je bois du thé.

_____

_____

Exercise 2

Now let's change it a little! Decide which negative phrase would be more appropriate from **ne** and **pas**, **ne** and **plus** and **ne** and **jamais**. Don't forget to change the **du**, **de la**, **des**, **de l'**, and **un**, **une**, **des** to **de** or **d'**.

1 Nous avons des cousins.

_____

2 Je voudrais du fromage.

_____

3 La famille a un chat dans la maison.

_____

4 J'ai un frère.

_____

5 Je voudrais de l'eau, s'il vous plaît.

_____

Exercise 3

Unfortunately, you usually only ever have jelly and ice cream in your house for dessert. Using **ne** and **jamais**, list some desserts you never have.

Note: Remember to revise your vocabulary on food to get the most benefit from this exercise!

> *Example:* Comme dessert, nous n'avons jamais de mousse au chocolat.

Exercise 4

You have recently become a vegetarian and have decided not to eat meat. Using **ne** and **plus**, list some five types of meat you no longer eat.

> *Example:* Je ne mange plus de porc.

12.7 The last word before we finish

In informal and familiar spoken French, **ne** is often dropped. These are some phrases you might use yourself or hear said in class:

Je ne sais pas.	⋯⋗ Je sais pas	*I don't know.*
Ne bouge pas !	⋯⋗ Bouge pas !	*Don't move!*
Ils ne sont pas encore arrivés.	⋯⋗ Ils sont pas encore arrivés. *They have not arrived yet.*	

Exercise 5
Allez-y !

Now let's have one final exercise before we finish. Your teacher is doing her Monday morning wake-up exercise of rapid-fire questions around the room. Be alert! Answer the following, using **ne** and **pas**, even if some of the sentences are true for you! Be careful of changes with the *indefinite* and *partitive* articles.

E.g. Tu as une gomme ?   Je n'ai pas de gomme.

1 Tu habites à Dublin ?   _____

2 Tu as un stylo ?   _____

3 Tu portes un uniforme ?   _____

4 Tu aimes la musique pop ?   _____

5 Tu joues au hurling ?   _____

6 Tu as une sœur ?   _____

7 Tu veux du chocolat ?   _____

8 Tu as un animal à la maison ?   _____

9 Il fait froid aujourd'hui ?   _____

10 Il pleut aujourd'hui ?   _____

12.8 The very last word – honestly!

Hopefully, you have found this chapter helpful. If you would like more information on using negatives in French, be sure to check out the chapters on the **passé composé** and on pronouns.

Now, hand on heart, answer the following questions truthfully!

Récapitulez

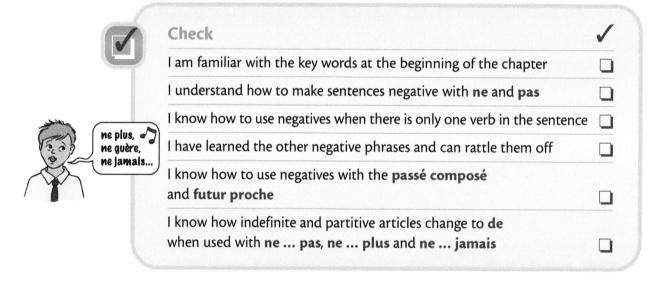

Check	✓
I am familiar with the key words at the beginning of the chapter	☐
I understand how to make sentences negative with **ne** and **pas**	☐
I know how to use negatives when there is only one verb in the sentence	☐
I have learned the other negative phrases and can rattle them off	☐
I know how to use negatives with the **passé composé** and **futur proche**	☐
I know how indefinite and partitive articles change to **de** when used with **ne … pas**, **ne … plus** and **ne … jamais**	☐

ne plus,
ne guère,
ne jamais...

Chapter 13
Discours Indirect
Indirect Speech

Key words

- Direct speech
- Indirect speech
- Reported speech
- Il/Elle dit de
- Il/Elle dit que
- Invert
- Il demande si
- Passé composé + imparfait = indirect speech in the past

13.1 A quick word before we begin

This chapter will be over before you know it. Blink and you'll miss it! So what is indirect speech? Well, firstly, let's just clarify what the opposite, *direct speech*, is.

> **Direct speech is really simple; the exact words of the speaker are written in quotes.**

Anna dit : « J'aime les frites. »	*Anna says, 'I like chips.'*
Eoin dit : « J'ai fait mes devoirs. »	*Eoin says, 'I have done my homework.'*

Rappel : Present tense of **demander** *(to ask)* and **dire** *(to say* or *to tell)*

Demander		Dire	
Je demande	nous demandons	Je dis	nous disons
tu demandes	vous demandez	tu dis	vous dites
il demande	ils demandent	il dit	ils disent
elle demande	elles demandent	elle dit	elles disent

Remember, both are **avoir** verbs in the **passé composé** and **dire** has an irregular past participle, **il a demandé** and **il a dit**.

13.2 Indirect speech and statements

> In *indirect speech*, the speaker's words are reported by somebody else and introduced by **que**.

Take a look at the examples on page 205, using *indirect speech* this time.

> Anna dit qu'elle aime les frites.

Did you notice how **j'aime** becomes **qu'elle aime** ? Anna says *that she likes* chips.

> Eoin dit qu'il a fait ses devoirs.

And **J'ai fait** changes to **qu'il a fait**. Eoin says *that he has done* his homework.

Somebody else is reporting his or her words. Is it any wonder, then, that *indirect speech* is also known as *reported speech*.

You will notice we use the example of **il dit** or **il demande** quite a lot in this chapter. This is just for simplicity. Obviously we may need to use other forms of the verb. We might just as easily be reporting what *they (girls) say* as what *she says*.

13.3 Using indirect speech to ask questions

If a question is introduced by a question word, such as **quand**, we put **il/elle demande** in front of the question word and *invert*, or turn around the verb and pronoun. Then, we slot in **est-ce que** after **quand** and voilà, we have made a question! **Il/elle demande** means *he/she asks/is asking*. Take a look:

> Quand sort-il avec ses amis ?   Elle demande quand est-ce qu'il sort avec ses amis.
> _____
> *When is he going out with his friends?*   *She asks when he is going out with his friends.*

Sort-il goes back to its original form of **il sort**.
She asks *when he is …*

13.4 Indirect speech and est-ce que ?

You know how you learned the phrase *est-ce que?* Remember how it turns a phrase into a question? Well, when you see this form of question, here's what you do:

> Est-ce que tu joues au rugby ? *Do you play rugby?*

> Take out **est-ce que** and put in **il/elle demande si**

> Arrête !
> Si+ il = s'il

> Il demande si tu joues au rugby. *He is asking if you play rugby.*
> Est-ce qu'il fait chaud aujourd'hui ? *Is it warm today?*
> ↓
> Elle demande s'il fait chaud aujourd'hui. *She is asking if it is warm today.*

13.5 Indirect speech and orders/imperatives

> Remember, the verb **dire** *to say* or *to tell* is followed by **à**. It takes an indirect object pronoun. You should check out the chapter on pronouns for more detail.

Note:

A note on the preposition de and à.
The preposition **de** or **à** is followed by a verb. This verb is always in the infinitive.

1 Ranges tes affaires ! *Tidy your things!*

> Elle lui dit de *ranger* ses affaires.
> _____
> *She tells him to tidy his things.*

See how the order, **ranges** *(tidy)*, changes to the *infinitive*, **ranger** *(to tidy)*, just like it would in English.

2 Fermez la porte ! *Shut the door!*

> Il leur dit de fermer la porte.
> _____
> *He tells them to shut the door.*

(Take a quick look at the chapter on pronouns)

Rappel ! Remember **lui** and **leur** are pronouns. We know if they are masculine or feminine by the context. The pictures here give us the context. In the first example, **elle lui dit … lui** refers to a boy. In the second, **il leur dit … leur** refers to a group of boys and girls.

13.6 Le passé composé and indirect speech

Let's really put indirect speech into practice. It's Monday morning and the topic of discussion is *the weekend*. What are the phrases you hear? Chances are they go something like: *he said that … she said that … and then we said that …* Here we need to use the **passé composé**. In the examples so far, there has been no change in tense because the statements are in the present.

What about when you want to report something that was said? We will just focus on indirect speech and *statements* with the **passé composé**. Really useful when you are catching up on the gossip and news!

Passé Composé + Imparfait = indirect speech
Main clause subordinate clause in the past
Il a dit que (what was said)

↓

again, **que** is the key word here, *he said that …*

Did you notice the changes in punctuation? You drop the colon: and the brackets « » when using indirect speech

Il a dit : « Je suis sorti avec Louise et Stephen. »

He said, 'I went out with Louise and Stephen.'

Il a dit qu'il sortait avec Louise et Stephen.

He said that he went out with Louise and Stephen.

Je suis sorti becomes … **qu'il sortait**

Elle a dit : « J'étais furieuse. »   *She said, 'I was furious.'*

Elle a dit qu'elle était furieuse.   *She said that she was furious.*

J'étais furieuse becomes … **qu'elle était furieuse**

And that is it!

Revision exercises

Now let's do some practice sentences using indirect speech.

Exercise 1
Indirect speech and the present tense

 Simply put **Il dit que**, **Ils disent que**, **Il demande si** or **il demande** before the following phrases, making changes as appropriate.

E.g. Je m'amuse. ⋯⟶ **Il dit qu'il** s'amuse.
     I enjoy myself.   *He says he is enjoying himself.*

1 Je vais au magasin.   *Il dit qu'*

_____

2 Je veux voir mon ami.

_____

3 Nous nous amusons bien.

_____

4 Tu fais les devoirs ?

_____

5 Finis tes devoirs !

_____

6 Répondez à toutes les questions.

_____

7 Nous allons danser.

_____

8 Nous sortons ce soir ?

_____

9 Est-ce que tu vas au cinéma ce soir ?

_____

10 Il va chez Paul.

_____

Indirect speech and the past tense

Exercise 2
Alan and Amy

Boîte de Vocabulaire:

un nouveau portable	*a new phone*
ravi	*delighted*
avoir de la chance	*to be lucky*
incroyable	*incredible*
furieux/euse	*furious (m) (f)*
rester chez …	*to stay with*

Alan is chatting with his friends and talking about his new gadget. He has been given an early birthday present. Can you write out the following sentences using *indirect speech* where needed?

- *He tells them that* the weekend was great.
- *His parents told him that* they bought him a new mobile phone for his birthday.
- *He told them that* he was delighted.
- *His dad told him that* he was very lucky.
- Amy is not impressed!
- Alan didn't phone her over the weekend.
- Unbelievable!
- *She told him that* she was furious.
- *He told her that* he was very busy.
- *He also told her* that his aunt and his cousins were staying at his house.
  Oh – oh!

Right, let's check!

Récapitulez

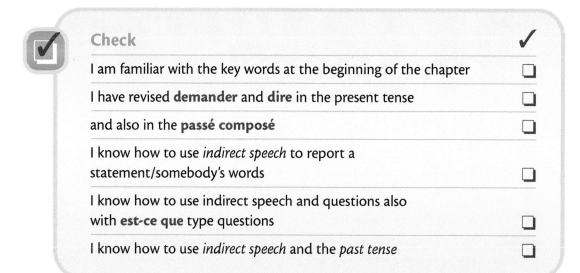

Check	✓
I am familiar with the key words at the beginning of the chapter	❑
I have revised **demander** and **dire** in the present tense	❑
and also in the **passé composé**	❑
I know how to use *indirect speech* to report a statement/somebody's words	❑
I know how to use indirect speech and questions also with **est-ce que** type questions	❑
I know how to use *indirect speech* and the *past tense*	❑

Chapter 14
Poser des Questions
Asking Questions

Key words

···⟡ Est-ce que ... ? ···⟡ N'est-ce pas ... ?

···⟡ Negative questions ···⟡ Oui/non/si

14.1 A quick word

Sometimes we tend to think life is all about ourselves. In a lot of the work you do in French, you are required to give information about yourself. However, it is not always about you, remember! You will also want to ask questions and find out information about other people.

You may simply want to find out someone's name, or you may be lost in Paris on a school tour! There are several ways of asking questions in French. The most basic of which is raising your voice at the end of a sentence, just like in English. However, this is maybe the easiest way to ask a question but it is only really used in spoken French.

Pour aller à la gare, s'il vous plaît ?

Où se trouve la boulangerie ?

To get maximum value out of this chapter, particularly for asking directions, you should revise your vocabulary on directions from your textbook.

14.2 **Use of a question mark**

Simply write the sentence and put a question mark at the end of it. If you were speaking, you would raise your voice at the end of the sentence. While this gets your point across, it is not formal enough for written work.

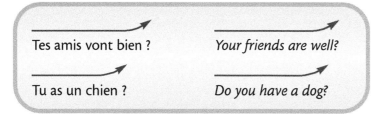

Tes amis vont bien ?   *Your friends are well?*

Tu as un chien ?   *Do you have a dog?*

14.3 **Est-ce que ?**

est-ce que, est-ce que, est-ce que...

Say it! Now say it again. This phrase is a little gem in French. Using it along with a question mark will turn a statement into a question and it is really easy to use. You don't need to change the order of the words in the sentence. Take a look:

> **Pronunciation**
> The letters **qu** together are pronounced with a k sound in French, e.g. **que**, **qui**, **qu'**, **quand**.

Tu joues au foot.   ⋯⋗   **Est-ce que** tu joues au foot ?
You play football or   *Do you play football?*
you are playing football

> The word order of the sentence hasn't changed. We have added in **est-ce que**, but the phrase **tu joues au foot** is still written the same way.

Tu vas au magasin.   ⋯⋗   Est-ce que tu vas au magasin ?

> Again, we are adding in **est-ce que**, but we are taking nothing away.

Rappel !

We must mention the *vowel* and *silent h*. No major issue here though.
Simply shorten the word **que** to **qu'**.

> Elle aime la musique. *She likes music.* ⋯⋮ Est-ce **qu'elle** aime la musique ?

Exercise 1

Using **est-ce que** or **est-ce-qu'**, turn these statements into questions:

1 Ton frère regarde le basket à la télé.

_____

2 Tu aimes l'anglais.

_____

3 Anna adore les chats.

_____

4 Ils écoutent le professeur.

_____

5 Suzanne habite à Longford.

_____

6 Tu as des frères et des sœurs.

_____

7 Vous allez à l'école en voiture.

_____

8 Sa mère chante bien.

_____

9 Tu fais tes devoirs.

_____

10 Alex et Nicola jouent au tennis.

_____

14.4   **Questions without est-ce que ?**

In English, we tend to change the word order of the sentence quite a bit. Instead of saying *you are going,* we make it a question by saying *are you going?* Instead of saying *you have brothers and sisters,* we say, *do you have brothers and sisters?* In French, we can do the same. Just join the verb and the pronoun together with a hyphen.

You have brothers and sisters.	⋯⋗	*Do you have brothers and sisters?*
You go to school.	⋯⋗	*Are you going to school?*

Or in French:		
Tu as des frères et des sœurs.	⋯⋗	As-tu des frères et des sœurs ?
Tu vas à l'école.	⋯⋗	Vas-tu à l'école ?

Sometimes you need to put in an extra **t** to make the pronunciation simpler. This is done in the third person singular (**il/elle/on**) if the verb ends in a vowel.

Take a look:

A-t-il un chien?

Mange-t-elle des légumes?

Il a un chien	⋯⋗	A-**t**-il un chien ?
Il mange des légumes.	⋯⋗	mange – t-elle des légumes ?
She eats vegetables.	⋯⋗	*Does she eat vegetables?*
Elle finira ses examens bientôt.	⋯⋗	Finira-t-elle ses examens bientôt ?
She will finish her exams soon.	⋯⋗	*Will she finish her exams soon?*
On arrivera en voiture.	⋯⋗	Arrivera-t-on en voiture ?
We will arrive by car.	⋯⋗	*Will we arrive by car?*

In the **passé composé**, you change the word order of the helping verb and the subject.

Tu as mangé des frites.	⋯⋙	As-tu mangé des frites ?
He ate chips.	⋯⋙	*Did he eat chips?*
Tu as regardé la télé.	⋯⋙	As-tu regardé la télé ?
You watched television.	⋯⋙	*Did you watch television?*
Elles sont sorties hier soir.	⋯⋙	Sont-elles sorties hier soir ?
They went out yesterday evening.	⋯⋙	*Did they go out yesterday evening?*

So that fits together very neatly! However, we don't always have the perfect situation. What about when we have a person's name instead of a pronoun?

Here's what happens:
Using a noun (e.g. Seán instead of **il**)

Seán sort avec ses amis.	⋯⋙	Seán sort-il avec ses amis ?

We leave what was said but add in a matching pronoun.

Sarah cherche son portefeuille.	⋯⋙	Sarah cherche-**t**-elle son portefeuille ?
Sarah is looking for her wallet.	⋯⋙	*Is Sarah looking for her wallet?*

And if necessary, we add in the **t** for pronunciation when we have a vowel at the end of the verb, followed by a pronoun beginning with a vowel.

Ta sœur regarde le film.	⋯⋙	Ta sœur regarde-t-elle le film ?
Your sister is watching the film.	⋯⋙	*Is your sister watching the film?*

Or in the **passé composé**:

Ta sœur a regardé le film.	⋯⋙	Ta sœur a-t-elle regardé le film ?
Your sister watched the film.	⋯⋙	*Did your sister watch the film?*

14.5 Using n'est-ce pas ?

You can turn a sentence into a question by putting in the phrase **n'est-ce pas** ?
at the end of the sentence. It can be translated in a few ways in English. Usually,
the phrase means *isn't that so?* or *won't you/he etc?* in English.

Il est malade, n'est-ce pas ?	*He is sick, isn't that so?*
Tu habites à la campagne, n'est-ce pas ?	*You live in the country, isn't that so?*
Ils viendront, n'est-ce pas ?	*They will come, won't they?*
Tu as fait tes devoirs, n'est-ce pas ?	*You did your homework, isn't that so?*

14.6 Negative questions

Using **ne** and **pas**, we can ask a question in a negative way.

Tu ne vas pas à l'école ?	*Are you not going to school?*
Ne vas-tu pas au cinéma ?	*Aren't you going to the cinema?*

14.7 Common question words

Don't forget that there are words such as *when* and *where* which also introduce a
question. These are the most common ones in French:

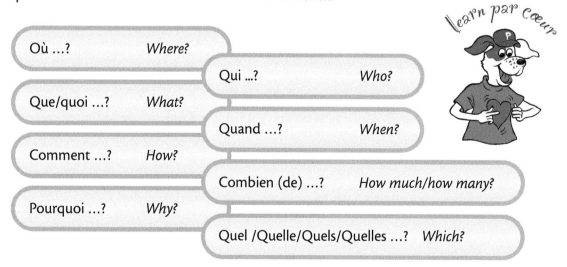

Où ...?	Where?
Qui ...?	Who?
Que/quoi ...?	What?
Quand ...?	When?
Comment ...?	How?
Combien (de) ...?	How much/how many?
Pourquoi ...?	Why?
Quel /Quelle/Quels/Quelles ...?	Which?

Exercise 2

Fill in the gaps with the common question words.

1 Tu as _____ de cousins ?

2 _____ est-ce que tu habites ?

3 Tu fais_____ de matières ?

4 _____ se trouve ta maison ?

5 _____ est l'anniversaire de ton père ?

6 _____ s'appelle ton prof de français ?

7 _____ va-t-elle faire l'année prochaine ?

8 _____ allez-vous à l'école ?

9 _____ restaurants est-ce qu'elles aiment ?

10 _____ voiture voudrais-tu ?

14.8 Answers with oui/non/si

Sometimes you will not be giving full answers to questions. Instead, you will simply be using

oui	*yes*
non	*no*

or si *yes*

Si is a special kind of word. We tend to associate it more with Spanish, but it is also used in French. It means *yes* in answer to a negative question. Take a look at some examples:

Est-ce que tu vas au cinéma ? *Oui !*	*Are you going to the cinema?* *Yes!*
Tu ne vas pas au cinéma ? *Si !*	*You're not going to the cinema?* *Yes!*
Ne vas-tu pas au cinéma ? *Si !*	*Aren't you going to the cinema?* *Yes!*

14.9 Special study: Asking for directions

This is when you will be asking questions a lot!

To get the best value out of this exercise, give yourself a quick vocabulary test on directions from your textbook. You should also revise buildings and shops.

Let's do some quick warm-up exercises. Read the conversations and answer the questions that follow.

Exercise 3

Anna is in France and has a sore throat. She wants to find a chemist to buy some lozenges.

1 Pardon monsieur, il y a une pharmacie près d'ici ?
- Oui, il y a une pharmacie avenue Curie.
- C'est loin ?
- Non, ce n'est pas loin. Tournez à droite et c'est après la gare.
- Merci monsieur.
- De rien.

Ms. Cassidy, who is on a school tour to Paris with her students, is trying to find the train station.

2 Pardon, madame. Où est la gare ?
- La gare se trouve avenue Carmel.
- C'est près d'ici ?
- C'est à cinq minutes à pied d'ici.
- Merci Madame

Conversation 1:

1 What is Anna looking for?

_____

2 Explain, in as much detail as you can, the directions given.

_____

_____

Conversation 2:

1 Where is Ms. Cassidy looking for?

_____

2 Explain, in as much detail you can, the directions given.

_____

_____

Exercise 4

Now can you make up some mini-dialogues of your own, based on looking for directions? You should ask about the way to go, using a selection of questions, e.g. *pour aller à, où se trouve …*

Now, using two question forms for each one, can you change the following sentences into questions? The verbs are in the **présent**.

1 Tu a un chien.

_____

_____

2 Leurs parents vont bien.

_____

_____

3 Il a des frères.

_____

_____

4 Tu aimes la danse.

_____

_____

5 Ils vont en France.

_____

_____

6 Vous êtes l'aîné de la famille.

_____

_____

7 Elle aide ses parents à la maison.

_____

_____

8 La boulangerie est près d'ici.

_____

_____

9 Tes parents aiment voyager.

_____

_____

10 Vous pouvez m'aider à faire mes devoirs.

_____

_____

Let's check!

Récapitulez

Check	✔
I am familiar with the key terms at the beginning of the chapter	☐
I know how to ask questions in spoken French	☐
I know how to use **est-ce que**	☐
I can ask questions without **est-ce que**	☐
I can understand the use of **n'est-ce pas**	☐
and negative questions	☐
I know how to use the common question words	☐
I am aware of how **si** is used in French	☐
I have revised my directions and how to ask the way in French	☐

French Phrases for Holidays

Any of you who have been to France have probably made a good effort with some basic French phrases. If you haven't, make sure you do next time!
The French really like it when visitors to the country make an effort with the language. Sometimes in France you may be really enthusiastic to speak, but find that you cannot put together the complete phrase. If you are going on holidays to France, or a French-speaking country soon, make sure to bring this simple guide of ready-to-use phrases with you.

Here are the magic phrases to get you out of those tricky situations!

Bon courage !

When you don't understand something

Je ne comprends pas.	*I don't understand.*
Parlez plus lentement, s'il vous plaît.	*Please speak slower.*
J'ai oublié le mot pour …	*I've forgotten the word for …*
Comment dit-on cela en français ?	*How do you say that in French?*
Voulez-vous répéter cela, s'il vous plaît ?	*Can you repeat that, please?*

Looking for directions/finding the way

Où se trouve la pharmacie/la banque/le restaurant/le cinéma, s'il vous plaît ?
Where is the chemist/bank/restaurant/cinema, please?

C'est à gauche.	*It's on the left.*
C'est à droite.	*It's on the right.*
Tout droit.	*Straight ahead.*
Le parc est loin d'ici	*The park is far from here.*
Le supermarché n'est pas loin d'ici	*The supermarket is not far from here.*

Le commissariat de police est à côté de l'église.
The police station is beside the church.

At your hotel

Quel est le prix de la chambre par nuit ?
What is the cost of the room per night?

On compte rester sept nuits.	*We will be staying for seven nights.*

L'hôtel ferme à quelle heure, le soir ?
What time does the hotel close in the evening?

Le petit déjeuner est servi à quelle heure ?	*Breakfast is served at what time?*
Je voudrais des serviettes, s'il vous plaît.	*I would like some towels, please.*

At the campsite

Avez-vous un emplacement de libre pour une caravane ?
Do you have space available for a caravan?

Avez-vous de la place pour une tente ?	*Do you have room for a tent?*

Nous voudrions rester jusqu'à samedi prochain.
We would like to stay until next Saturday.

Où est le bloc sanitaire ?	*Where is the toilet/shower block?*

Y a-t-il un supermarché dans le terrain de camping ?
Is there a supermarket on site?

At the doctors

Je ne me sens pas bien.	*I don't feel well.*
Je me sens malade.	*I feel sick.*
J'ai mal à la tête.	*I have a headache.*
J'ai mal au ventre.	*I have stomach ache.*
J'ai de la fièvre.	*I have a fever.*
J'ai la tête qui tourne.	*I feel dizzy.*
Depuis trois jours, je tousse.	*I've been coughing for three days.*

At the chemist

Je voudrais des pansements/des pastilles, s'il vous plaît.
I would like some plasters/throat lozenges please.

Avez-vous quelque chose pour le rhume ?
Do you have anything for a cold?

J'ai pris un coup de soleil.
I have sunburn

Je suis allergique à la pénicilline.
I'm allergic to penicillin.

When you lose something/when something is stolen

Vous devez aller au commissariat de police.	*You have to go to the police station.*
J'ai perdu mon passeport.	*I've lost my passport.*
On m'a volé mon sac.	*My bag has been stolen.*
Il y avait un appareil-photo dedans.	*There was a camera inside it.*

Travel

Le prochain train pour Bordeaux part à quelle heure.
When does the next train for Bordeaux leave.

A quelle heure est-ce qu'il arrive ?
What time does it arrive?

Un aller-simple pour Lyon, s'il vous plaît.
A single ticket for Lyon, please.

Un aller-retour pour Nice, s'il vous plaît.
A return ticket for Nice, please.

Le train part de quel quai ?
What platform does the train leave from?

Est-ce qu'il y a un car qui va à l'aéroport ?
Is there a coach to the airport?

A quelle heure part le prochain vol pour Dublin ?
What time does the next plane for Dublin leave at?

Restaurants and cafés

Avez-vous une table pour cinq ?	*Have you a table for five, please?*
Je voudrais commander maintenant ?	*I would like to order now, please?*
Comme hors-d'œuvre, je voudrais …	*To start, I would like …*
Comme plat principal, je prendrai …	*For the main course, I will take …*
Comme dessert, nous voudrions …	*For desert, we would like …*
Comme boisson, je prendrai …	*To drink, I will take …*
L'addition, s'il vous plaît …	*The bill, please …*

Common Irregular Verbs

Now let's take a look at your store of verbs. These are the most common irregular verbs you will come across. Learn by heart!

Infinitif	Présent	Passé Composé	Imparfait	Futur	Conditionnel
Aller *To go*	je vais	je suis allé(e)	j'allais	j'irai	j'irais
	tu vas	tu es allé(e)	tu allais	tu iras	tu irais
	il/elle/on va	il/on est allé	il/elle/on allait	Il/elle/on ira	il/elle/on irait
	nous allons	elle est allée	nous allions	nous irons	nous irions
	vous allez	nous sommes allé(e)s	vous alliez	vous irez	vous iriez
	ils/elles vont	vous êtes allé (e)(s)	ils/elles allaient	Ils/elles iront	ils/elles iraient
		ils sont allés			
		elles sont allées			
Avoir *To have*	j'ai	j'ai eu	j'avais	j'aurai	j'aurais
	tu as	tu as eu	tu avais	tu auras	tu aurais
	il/elle/on a	il/elle/on a eu	il/elle/on avait	Il/elle/on aura	Il/elle aurait
	nous avons	nous avons eu	nous avions	nous aurons	nous aurions
	vous avez	vous avez eu	vous aviez	vous aurez	vous auriez
	ils/elles ont	ils/elles ont eu	ils/elles avaient	ils/elles auront	ils/elles auraient

Infinitif	Présent	Passé Composé	Imparfait	Futur	Conditionnel
Boire *To drink*	je bois tu bois Il/elle/on boit nous buvons vous buvez ils/elles boivent	j'ai bu tu as bu il/elle/on a bu nous avons bu vous avez bu ils/elles ont bu	je buvais tu buvais il/elle/on buvait nous buvions vous buviez ils/elles buvaient	je boirai tu boiras il/elle/on boira nous boirons vous boirez ils/elles boiront	je boirais tu boirais il/elle/on boirait nous boirions vous boiriez ils/elles boiraient

Connaître
*To know
people/
places*
	je connais
	tu connais
	il/elle/on connaît
	nous connaissons
	vous connaissez
	ils/elles
	    connaissent
		j'ai connu
		tu as connu
		il/elle/on a connu
		nous avons connu
		vous avez connu
		ils/elles ont connu
			je connaissais
			tu connaissais
			il/elle/on
			    connaissait
			nous connaissions
			vous connaissiez
			ils/elles
			    connaissient
				je connaîtrai
				tu connaîtras
				il/elle/on
				    connaîtra
				nous connaîtrons
				vous connaîtrez
				ils/elles
				    connaîtront
					je connaîtrais
					tu connaîtrais
					il/elle/on
					    connaîtrait
					nous connaîtrions
					vous connaîtriez
					ils/elles
					    connaîtraient

Devoir *To have to (must)*	je dois tu dois il/elle/on doit nous devons vous devez ils doivent elles doivent	j'ai dû tu as dû il/elle/on a dû nous avons dû vous avez dû ils/elles ont dû	je devais tu devais il/elle/on devait nous devions vous deviez ils/elles devaient	je devrai tu devras il/elle/on devra nous devrons vous devrez ils/elles devront	je devrais tu devrais il/elle/on devrait nous devrions vous devriez ils/elles devraient

Infinitif	Présent	Passé Composé	Imparfait	Futur	Conditionnel
Être *To be*	je suis tu es il/elle/on est nous sommes vous êtes ils sont elles sont	j'ai été tu as été il/elle/on a été nous avons été vous avez été ils/elles ont été	j'étais tu étais il/elle/on était nous étions vous étiez ils/elles étaient	je serai tu seras il/elle/on sera nous serons vous serez ils/elles seront	je serais tu serais il/elle/on serait nous serions vous seriez ils/elles seraient
Faire *To do/ to make*	je fais tu fais il/elle/on fait nous faisons vous faites ils font elles font	j'ai fait tu as fait Il/elle/on a fait nous avons fait vous avez fait ils ont fait elles ont fait	je faisais tu faisais il/elle/on faisait nous faisions vous faisiez ils/elles faisaient	je ferai tu feras il/elle/on fera nous ferons vous ferez ils/elles feront	je ferais tu ferais il/elle/on ferait nous ferions vous feriez ils/elles feraient
Mettre *To put*	je mets tu mets il/elle/on met nous mettons vous mettez ils/elles mettent	j'ai mis tu as mis il/elle/on a mis nous avons mis vous avez mis ils/elles ont mis	je mettais tu mettais il/elle/on mettait nous mettions vous mettiez ils/elles mettaient	je mettrai tu mettras il/elle/on mettra nous mettrons vous mettrez ils/elles mettront	je mettrais tu mettrais il/elle mettrait nous mettrions vous mettriez ils/elles mettraient

Infinitif	Présent	Passé Composé	Imparfait	Futur	Conditionnel

Partir *To leave/ to depart*	je pars
	tu pars
	il/elle/on part
	nous partons
	vous partez
	ils/elles partent
		je suis parti(e)
		tu es parti(e)
		il/on est parti
		elle est partie
		nous sommes
		  parti(e)(s)
		vous êtes
		  parti(e) (s)
		ils sont partis
		elles sont parties
			je partais
			tu partais
			il/elle/on partait
			nous partions
			vous partiez
			ils/elles partaient
				je partirai
				tu partiras
				il/elle/on partira
				nous partirons
				vous partirez
				ils/elles partiront
					je partirais
					tu partirais
					il/elle/on partirait
					nous partirions
					vous partiriez
					ils/elles partiraient

Pouvoir *To be able to*	je peux tu peux il/elle/on peut nous pouvons vous pouvez ils/elles peuvent	j'ai pu tu as pu il/elle/on a pu nous avons pu vous avez pu ils/elles ont pu	je pouvais tu pouvais il/elle/on pouvait nous pouvions vous pouviez ils/elles pouvaient	je pourrai tu pourras il/elle/on pourra nous pourrons vous pourrez ils/elles pourront	je pourrais tu pourrais il/elle/on pourrait nous pourrions vous pourriez ils/elles pourraient

Prendre *To take*	je prends
	tu prends
	il/elle/on prend
	nous prenons
	vous prenez
	ils/elles prennent
		j'ai pris
		tu as pris
		il/elle/on a pris
		nous avons pris
		vous avez pris
		ils/elles ont pris
			je prenais
			tu prenais
			il/elle/on prenait
			nous prenions
			vous preniez
			ils/elles prenaient
				je prendrai
				tu prendras
				il/elle/on prendra
				nous prendrons
				vous prendrez
				ils/elles prendront
					je prendrais
					tu prendrais
					il/elle/on
					  prendrait
					nous prendrions
					vous prendriez
					ils/elles
					  prendraient

Infinitif	Présent	Passé Composé	Imparfait	Futur	Conditionnel
Recevoir *To get/ to receive*	je reçois tu reçois il/elle/on reçoit nous recevons vous recevez ils/elles reçoivent	j'ai reçu tu as reçu il/elle/on a reçu nous avons reçu vous avez reçu Ils/elles ont reçu	je recevais tu recevais il/elle/on recevait nous recevions vous receviez Ils/elles recevaient	je recevrai tu recevras il/elle/on recevra nous recevrons vous recevrez ils/elles recevront	je recevrais tu recevrais il/elle/on recevrait nous recevrions vous recevriez ils/elles recevraient
Savoir *To know (information/ knowledge)*	je sais tu sais il/elle/on sait nous savons vous savez ils/elles savent	j'ai su tu as su il/elle/on a su nous avons su vous avez su ils/elles ont su	je savais tu savais Il/elle/on savait nous savions vous saviez ils/elles savaient	je saurai tu sauras il/elle/on saura nous saurons vous saurez ils/elles sauront	je saurais tu saurais il/elle/on saurait nous saurions vous sauriez ils/elles sauraient
Sortir *To go out*	je sors tu sors il/elle/on sort nous sortons vous sortez ils/elles sortent	je suis sorti(e) tu es sorti(e) il/on est sorti elle est sortie nous sommes sorti(e)(s) vous êtes sorti(e)(s) ils sont sortis elles sont sorties	je sortais tu sortais il/elle/on sortait nous sortions vous sortiez ils/elles sortaient	je sortirai tu sortiras il/elle/on sortira nous sortirons vous sortirez ils/elles sortiront	je sortirais tu sortirais il/elle/on sortirait nous sortirions vous sortiriez ils/elles sortiraient

Infinitif	Présent	Passé Composé	Imparfait	Futur	Conditionnel

Venir
To come
	je viens
	tu viens
	il/elle/on vient
	nous venons
	vous venez
	ils/elles viennent
		je suis venu(e)
		tu es venu (e)
		il/on est venu
		elle est venue
		nous sommes
		  venu(e)(s)
		vous êtes
		  venu(e)(s)
		ils sont venus
		elles sont venues
			je venais
			tu venais
			il/elle/on venait
			nous venions
			vous veniez
			ils/elles venaient
				je viendrai
				tu viendras
				il/elle/on viendra
				nous viendrons
				vous viendrez
				ils/elles viendront
					je viendrais
					tu viendrais
					il/elle/on viendrait
					nous viendrions
					vous viendriez
					ils/elles viendraient

Voir *To see*	je vois tu vois il/elle/on voit nous voyons vous voyez ils/elles voient	j'ai vu tu as vu il/elle/on a vu nous avons vu vous avez vu ils/elles ont vu	je voyais tu voyais il/elle/on voyait nous voyions vous voyiez ils/elles voyaient	je verrai tu verras il/elle/on verra nous verrons vous verrez ils/elles verront	je verrais tu verrais il/elle/on verrait nous verrions vous verriez ils/elles verraient
Vouloir *To want/ wish*	je veux tu veux il/elle/on veut nous voulons vous voulez Ils/elles veulent	j'ai voulu tu as voulu il/elle/on a voulu nous avons voulu vous avez voulu ils/elles ont voulu	je voulais tu voulais il/elle/on voulait nous voulions vous vouliez ils/elles voulaient	je voudrai tu voudras il/elle/on voudra nous voudrons vous voudrez ils/elles voudront	je voudrais tu voudrais il/elle/on voudrait nous voudrions vous voudriez ils/elles voudraient

Vocabulary Hints

Use the following vocabulary to help you complete the exercises.

1 Les animaux *animals*

Le cheval	*horse*	Le lapin	*rabbit*
Le chien	*dog*	La souris	*mouse*
Le chat	*cat*	La tortue	*tortoise*

2 Les bâtiments et les magasins *buildings and shops*

La banque	*bank*	Le musée	*museum*
La bibliothèque	*library*	L'office du tourisme	*tourist office*
La boulangerie	*baker's*	Le parc	*park*
Le café	*café*	La pharmacie	*chemist's*
Le cinéma	*cinema*	La piscine	*swimming pool*
L'école primaire	*primary school*	La poste	*post office*
La gare	*station*	Le supermarché	*supermarket*
La gare routière	*train station*	Le syndicat d'initiative	*tourist information office*
Le lycée	*secondary school*		

3 Les boissons *drinks*

Le chocolat chaud	*hot chocolate*	Le jus d'orange	*orange juice*
Le lait	*milk*	Le thé	*tea*

4 Le cartable/la trousse *schoolbag/pencil case*

Le stylo	*pen*	Le crayon	*pencil*
Le carnet	*notebook*	La calculatrice	*calculator*
Le taille-crayon	*sharpner*	Le compas	*compass*
Le classeur	*folder*	Le cahier	*copy*
L'agenda	*diary/school journal*	Le feutre	*marker*
Le livre	*book*	La gomme	*rubber*

5 Le corps *the body*

L'oeil/ les yeux	*eye/eyes*	Le ventre	*stomach*
L'oreille	*ear*	Le genou	*knee*
Le menton	*chin*	Le dos	*back*
L'épaule	*shoulder*	La cheville	*ankle*
La poitrine	*chest*	Le pied	*foot*

6 La cuisine *the kitchen*

Le buffet	*sideboard*	Le frigo	*fridge*
La chaise	*chair*	Le lave-vaisselle	*dishwasher*
La cuisinière	*cooker*	Le micro-onde	*microwave*
Le congélateur	*freezer*	Les placards	*presses*
L'évier	*sink*	La table	*table*

7   Les matières *subjects*

L'allemand	German	L'éducation civique	C.S.P.E
L'anglais	English	L'éducation physique	physical education
Les arts ménagers	home economics	Le français	French
La biologie	biology	Le gaélique	Irish language
Le commerce	business studies	La géographie	geography
La chimie	chemistry	L'histoire	history
Le dessin	art/drawing	Les maths	maths
Le dessin technique	technical drawing	La physique	physics

8   La nourriture *food*

Le beurre	butter	Le pain	bread
Les céréales	cereal	Le fromage	cheese
La confiture	jam		
Les légumes	**vegetables**		
Le chou	cabbage	Les petits pois	peas
Les frites	chips	La pomme de terre	potatoe
Les oignons	onions		
La banane	banana	La framboise	raspberry
La fraise	strawberry	Le raisin	grape
Les desserts	**desserts**		
Les crêpes	pancakes	La salade de fruits	fruit salad
La mousse au chocolat	chocolate mousse	Le sorbet	sorbet
La viande	**meat**		
L'agneau	lamb	Le poulet	chicken
Le bœuf	beef	Le steak	steak
Le jambon	ham	Le veau	veal
Le mouton	mutton		

9   Les passe-temps *hobbies*

Jouer de la guitare/ de la batterie	*playing the guitar/drums*	La peinture	*painting*
La danse	*dancing*	Surfer sur le Net	*surf the Internet*
La lecture	*reading*	Télécharger de la musique	*download music*

10   La salle de classe *the classroom*

La brosse	*duster*	L'ordinateur	*computer*
La carte	*map*	Le placard	*press*
Les étagères	*shelves*	Le poster	*poster*
L'horloge	*clock*	La poubelle	*bin*

11   Le sport *sport*

Le badminton	*badminton*	Le hockey	*hockey*
Le basket	*basketball*	Le hurling	*hurling*
Le camogie	*camogie*	Le rugby	*rugby*
Le football	*soccer*	Le tennis	*tennis*
Le football gaélique	*gaelic football*		

12   Les vêtements *clothes*

Les baskets	*runners*	Le manteau	*coat*
La chemise	*shirt*	Le pantalon	*trousers*
Les bottes	*boots*	Le survêtement	*tracksuit*
La ceinture	*belt*	Les tongs	*filp-flops*
Le jean	*jeans*	La veste	*jacket*
La jupe	*skirt*		